The Trial and of Jesus Christ

A Devotional History of Our Lord's Passion

James Stalker

Alpha Editions

This edition published in 2024

ISBN : 9789362096357

Design and Setting By
Alpha Editions
www.alphaedis.com
Email - info@alphaedis.com

As per information held with us this book is in Public Domain.
This book is a reproduction of an important historical work. Alpha Editions uses the best technology to reproduce historical work in the same manner it was first published to preserve its original nature. Any marks or number seen are left intentionally to preserve its true form.

Contents

PREFACE ....- 1 -
CHAPTER I. ....- 3 -
CHAPTER II. ....- 9 -
CHAPTER III. ....- 16 -
CHAPTER IV. ....- 23 -
CHAPTER V. ....- 30 -
CHAPTER VI. ....- 36 -
CHAPTER VII. ....- 43 -
CHAPTER VIII. ....- 49 -
CHAPTER IX. ....- 55 -
CHAPTER X. ....- 62 -
CHAPTER XI. ....- 68 -
CHAPTER XII. ....- 74 -
CHAPTER XIII. ....- 82 -
CHAPTER XIV. ....- 88 -
CHAPTER XV ....- 94 -
CHAPTER XVI. ....- 101 -
CHAPTER XVII. ....- 107 -
CHAPTER XVIII ....- 114 -
CHAPTER XIX. ....- 120 -
CHAPTER XX ....- 125 -
CHAPTER XXI. ....- 131 -
CHAPTER XXII. ....- 138 -
CHAPTER XXIII ....- 144 -

PREFACE

Ever since I wrote, in a contracted form, *The Life of Jesus Christ*, the desire has slumbered in my mind to describe on a much more extended scale the closing passages of the Saviour's earthly history; and, although renewed study has deepened my sense of the impossibility of doing these scenes full justice, yet the subject has never ceased to attract me, as being beyond all others impressive and remunerative.

The limits of our Lord's Passion are somewhat indeterminate. Krummacher begins with the Triumphal Entry into Jerusalem, Tauler with the Feet-washing before the Last Supper, and Rambach with Gethsemane; most end with the Death and Burial; but Grimm, a Roman Catholic, the latest writer on the subject, means to extend his *Leidensgeschichte* to the end of the Forty Days. Taking the word "passion" in the strict sense, I have commenced at the point where, by falling into the hands of His enemies, our Lord was deprived of voluntary activity; and I have finished with the Burial. No doubt the same unique greatness belongs to the scenes of the previous evening; and I should like to write of Christ among His Friends as I have here written of Him among His Foes; but for this purpose a volume at least as large as the present one would be requisite; and the portion here described has an obvious unity of its own.

The bibliography of the Passion is given with considerable fulness in Zöckler's *Das Kreuz Christi*; but a good many of the books there enumerated may be said to have been superseded by the monumental work of Nebe, *Die Leidensgeschichte unsers Herrn Hesu Christi* (2 vols., 1881), which, though not a work of genius, is written on so comprehensive a plan and with such abundance of learning that nothing could better serve the purpose of anyone who wishes to draw the skeleton before painting the picture. Of the numerous Lives of Christ those by Keim and Edersheim are worthy of special notice in this part of the history, because of the fulness of information from classical sources in the one and from Talmudical in the other. Steinmeyer (*Leidensgeschichte*) is valuable on apologetic questions. On the Seven Words from the Cross there is an extensive special literature. Schleiermacher and Tholuck are remarkably good; and there are volumes by Baring-Gould, Scott Holland and others.

In the sub-title I have called this book a Devotional History, because the subject is one which has to be studied with the heart as well as the head. But I have not on this account written in the declamatory and interrogatory style common in devotional works. I have to confess that some even of the most famous books on the Passion are to me intolerably tedious, because they are written, so to speak, in oh's and ah's. Surely this is not essential to devotion. The scenes of the Passion ought, indeed, to stir the depths of the heart; but this purpose is best attained, not by the narrator displaying his own emotions, but, as is shown in the incomparable model of the Gospels, by the faithful exhibition of the facts themselves.

GLASGOW, 1894.

CHAPTER I.

THE ARREST

Our study of the closing scenes of the life of our Lord begins at the point where He fell into the hands of the representatives of justice; and this took place at the gate of Gethsemane and at the midnight hour.

On the eastern side of Jerusalem, the ground slopes downwards to the bed of the Brook Kedron; and on the further side of the stream rises the Mount of Olives. The side of the hill was laid out in gardens or orchards belonging to the inhabitants of the city; and Gethsemane was one of these. There is no probability that the enclosure now pointed out to pilgrims at the foot of the hill is the actual spot, or that the six aged olive trees which it contains are those to the silent shadows of which the Saviour used to resort; but the scene cannot have been far away, and the piety which lingers with awe in the traditional site cannot be much mistaken.

The agony in Gethsemane was just over, when "lo," as St. Matthew says, "Judas, one of the twelve, came, and with him a great multitude." They had come down from the eastern gate of the city and were approaching the entrance to the garden. It was full moon, and the black mass was easily visible, moving along the dusty road.

The arrest of Christ was not made by two or three common officers of justice. The "great multitude" has to be taken literally, but not in the sense of a disorderly crowd. As it was at the instance of the ecclesiastical authorities that the apprehension took place, their servants—the Levitical police of the temple—were to the front. But, as Jesus had at least eleven resolute men with Him, and these might rouse incalculable numbers of His adherents on the way to the city, it had been considered judicious to ask from the Roman governor a division of soldiers,[1] which, at the time of the Passover, was located in the fortress of Antonia, overlooking the temple, to intervene in any emergency. And some of the members of the Sanhedrim had even come themselves, so eager were they to see that the design should not miscarry. This composite force was armed with swords and staves—the former weapon belonging perhaps to the Roman soldiers and the latter to the temple police—and they carried lanterns and torches, probably because they expected to have to hunt for Jesus and His followers in the recesses of His retreat. Altogether it was a formidable body: they were determined to make assurance doubly sure.

I.

The leader of them was Judas. Of the general character of this man, and the nature of his crime, enough will be said later; but here we must note that there were special aggravations in his mode of carrying out his purpose.

He profaned the Passover. The better day, says the proverb, the better deed. But, if a deed is evil, it is the worse if it is done on a sacred day. The Passover was the most sacred season of the entire year; and this very evening was the most sacred of the Passover week. It was as if a crime should in Scotland be committed by a member of the Church on the night of a Communion Sabbath, or in England on Christmas Day.

He invaded the sanctuary of his Master's devotions. Gethsemane was a favourite resort of Jesus; Judas had been there with Him, and he knew well for what purpose He frequented it. But the respect due to a place of prayer did not deter him; on the contrary, he took advantage of his Master's well-known habit.

But the crowning profanation, for which humanity will never forgive him, was the sign by which he had agreed to make his Master known to His enemies. It is probable that he came on in front, as if he did not belong to the band behind; and, hurrying towards Jesus, as if to apprise Him of His danger and condole with Him on so sad a misfortune as His apprehension, he flung himself on His neck, sobbing, "Master, Master!" and not only did he kiss Him, but he did so repeatedly or fervently: so the word signifies.[2] As long as there is true, pure love in the world, this act will be hated and despised by everyone who has ever given or received this token of affection. It was a sin against the human heart and all its charities. But none can feel its horror as it must have been felt by Jesus. That night and the next day His face was marred in many ways: it was furrowed by the bloody sweat; it was bruised with blows; they spat upon it; it was rent with thorns: but nothing went so close to His heart as the profanation of this kiss. As another said, who had been similarly treated: "It was not an enemy that reproached me, then I could have borne it; neither was it he that hated me that did magnify himself against me, then I would have hid myself from him; but it was thou, a man mine equal, my guide and mine acquaintance; we took sweet counsel together, and walked to the house of God in company." [3] Before the kiss was given, Jesus still received him with the old name of Friend; but, after being stung with it, He could not keep back the annihilating question, "Judas, betrayest thou the Son of man with a kiss?"

The kiss was the sign of discipleship. In the East, students used to kiss their rabbis; and in all likelihood this custom prevailed between Christ and His disciples. When we become His disciples, we may be said to kiss Him; and every time we renew the pledge of our loyalty we may be said to repeat this act. We do so especially in the Lord's Supper. In our baptism He may be said to take us up in His arms and kiss us; in the other sacrament we obtain the opportunity of returning this mark of affection.

II.

Probably Judas, being ahead of the band he was leading, went somewhat into the shadows of the garden to reach Jesus; and no doubt it was expected that Jesus would try to get away. But, instead of doing so, He shook Himself free from Judas and, coming forward at once into the moonlight, demanded, "Whom seek ye?"

At this they were so startled that they reeled back and, stepping one on another, fell to the ground.

Similar incidents are related of famous men. The Roman Marius, for instance, was in prison at Minturnae when Sylla sent orders that he should be put to death. A Gaulish slave was sent to dispatch him; but, at the sight of the man who had shaken the world, and who cried out, "Fellow, darest thou to slay Caius Marius?" the soldier threw down his weapon and fled.[4]

There are many indications scattered through the Gospels that, especially in moments of high emotion, there was something extraordinarily subduing in the aspect and voice of Christ.[5] On the occasion, for example, when He cleared the temple, the hardened profaners of the place, though numerous and powerful, fled in terror before Him. And the striking notice of Him as He was going up to Jerusalem for the last time will be remembered: "Jesus went before them, and they were amazed; and, as they followed, they were afraid."

On this occasion the emotion of Gethsemane was upon Him—the rapt sense of victory and of a mind steeled to go through with its purpose—and perhaps there remained on His face some traces of the Agony, which scared the onlookers. It is not necessary to suppose that there was anything preternatural, though part of the terror of His captors may have been the dread lest He should destroy them by a miracle. Evidently Judas was afraid of something of this kind when he said, "Take Him and lead Him away safely."

The truth is, they were caught, instead of catching Him. It was a mean, treacherous errand they were on. They were employing a traitor as their guide. They expected to come upon Christ, perhaps when He was asleep, in silence and by stealth; or, if He were awake, they thought that they would have to pursue Him into a lurking-place, where they would find Him trembling and at bay. They were to surprise Him, but, when He came forth fearless, rapt and interrogative, He surprised them, and compelled them to take an altogether unexpected attitude. He brought all above board and put them to shame.

How ridiculous now looked their cumbrous preparations—all these soldiers, the swords and staves, the torches and lanterns, now burning pale in the clear moonlight. Jesus made them feel it. He made them feel what manner of spirit they were of, and how utterly they had mistaken His views and spirit. "Whom seek ye?" He asked them again, to compel them to see that they were not taking Him, but that He was giving Himself up. He was completely master of the situation. Singling out the Sanhedrists, who probably at that moment would rather have kept in the background, He demanded, pointing to their excessive preparations, "Be ye come out as against a thief, with swords and staves? When I was daily with you in the temple, ye stretched forth no hands against Me." He, a solitary man, though He knew how many were against Him, had not been afraid: He taught daily in the temple—in the most public place, at the most public hour. But they, numerous and powerful as they were, yet were afraid, and so they had chosen the midnight hour for their nefarious purpose. "This is your hour," He said, "and the power of darkness." This midnight hour is your hour, because ye are sons of night, and the power ye wield against Me is the power of darkness.

So spake the Lion of the tribe of Judah! So will He speak on that day when all His enemies shall be put under His feet. "Kiss the Son, lest He be angry, and ye perish from the way when His wrath is kindled but a little. Blessed are all they that put their trust in Him."

III.

We cannot recall to mind too often that it was the victory in the Garden that accounted for this triumph outside the gate. The irresistible dignity and strength here displayed were gained by watching and prayer.

This, however, is made still more impressively clear by the fate of those who did not watch and pray. On them everything came as a blinding and bewildering surprise. They were aroused out of profound slumber, and came stumbling forward hardly yet awake. When hands were laid on Jesus, one of the disciples cried, "Shall we smite with the sword?" And, without waiting for an answer, he struck. But what a ridiculous blow! How like a man half-awake! Instead of the head, he only smote the ear. This blow would have been dearly paid for had not Jesus, with perfect presence of mind, interposed between Peter and the swords which were being drawn to cut him down. "Suffer ye thus far," He said, keeping the soldiers back; and, touching the ear, He healed it, and saved His poor disciple.

Surely it was even with a smile that Jesus said to Peter, "Put up again thy sword into his place; for all they that take the sword shall perish with the sword." Inside the scabbard, not outside, was the sword's place; it was out of place in this cause; and those who wield the sword without just reason, and without receiving the orders of competent authority, are themselves liable to give life for life.

But it was with the high-strung eloquence with which He had spoken to His enemies that Jesus further showed Peter how inconsistent was his act. It was inconsistent with his Master's dignity; "For," said He, "if I ask My Father, He would presently give Me more than twelve legions of angels;" and what against such a force were this miscellaneous band, numbering at the most the tenth part of a legion of men? It was inconsistent with Scripture: "How then shall the Scriptures be fulfilled, that thus it must be?" It was inconsistent with His own purpose and His Father's will: "The cup which My Father hath given Me, shall I not drink it?"

Poor Peter! On this occasion he was thoroughly like himself. There was a kind of rightness and nobleness in what he did; but it was in the wrong place. If he had only been as prompt inside Gethsemane to do what he was bidden as outside it to do what he was not bidden! How much better if he could have drawn the spiritual sword and cut on the ear which was to be betrayed by a maid-servant's taunt! Peter's conduct on this occasion, as often on other occasions, showed how poor a guide enthusiasm is when it is not informed with the mind and spirit of Christ.

IV.

Perhaps it was by the recollection of how deeply he had vowed to stick by Christ, even if he should have to die with Him, that Peter was pricked on to do something. The others, however, had said the same thing. Did they remember it now? It is to be feared, not: the apparition of mortal danger drove everything out of their minds but the instinct of self-preservation. Sometimes, in cases of severe illness, especially of mental disease, the curious effect may be observed—that a face into which years of culture have slowly wrought the stamp of refinement and dignity entirely loses this, and reverts to the original peasant type. So the fright of their Master's arrest, coming so suddenly on the prayerless and unprepared disciples, undid, for the time, what their years of intercourse with Him had effected; and they sank back into Galilean fishermen again. This was really what they were from the arrest to the resurrection.

Here again their conduct is in absolute contrast with their Master's. As a mother-bird, when her brood is assailed, goes forward to meet the enemy, or as a good shepherd stands forth between his flock and danger, so Jesus, when His captors drew nigh, threw Himself between them and His followers. It was partly with this in view that He went so boldly out and concentrated attention on Himself by the challenge, "Whom seek ye?" When they replied,

"Jesus of Nazareth," He said, "I am He: if therefore ye seek Me, let these go their way." And the fright into which they were thrown made them forget His followers in their anxiety to secure Himself.

This was as He intended. St. John, in narrating it, makes the curious remark, that this was done that the saying might be fulfilled which He spake, "Of them which Thou gavest Me have I lost none." This saying occurs in His great intercessory prayer, offered at the first Communion table; but in its original place it evidently means that He had lost none of them in a spiritual sense, whereas here it seems to have only the sense of losing any of them by the swords of the soldiers or by the cross, if they had been arrested with Him. But a deep hint underlies this surface meaning. St. John suggests that, if any of them had been taken along with Him, the likelihood is that they would have been unequal to the crisis: they would have denied Him, and so, in the sadder sense, would have been lost.

Jesus, knowing too well that this was the state of the case, made for them a way of escape, and "they all forsook Him and fled." It was perhaps as well, for they might have done worse. Yet what an anticlimax to the asseveration which everyone of them had made that very evening, "If I should die with Thee, I will not deny Thee in any wise!" I have sometimes thought what an honour it would have been to Christianity, what a golden leaf in the history of human nature, had one or two of them—say, the brothers James and John—been strong enough to go with Him to prison and to death. We should, indeed, have missed St. John's writings in that case—his Revelation, Gospel and Epistles. But what a revelation that would have been, what a gospel, what a living epistle!

It was not, however, to be. Jesus had to go unaccompanied: "I have trodden the winepress alone; and of the people there was none with Me." So they "bound Him and led Him away."

[1] *Speira*=cohors, tenth part of legion. See Ramsay, R.A., 381.

[2] *katephilesen*. It is used of the woman who was a sinner, when she kissed the feet of the Saviour.

[3] Psalm lv. 13-14.

[4] Other instances in Süskind, *Passionsschule, in loc.*

[5] See fuller details in *Imago Christi*, last chapter.

CHAPTER II.

THE ECCLESIASTICAL TRIAL

Over the Kedron, up the slope to the city, through the gates, along the silent streets, the procession passed, with Jesus in the midst; midnight stragglers, perhaps, hurrying forward from point to point to ask what was ado, and peering towards the Prisoner's face, before they diverged again towards their own homes.[1] He was conducted to the residence of the high priest, where His trial ensued.

Jesus had to undergo two trials—the one ecclesiastical, the other civil; the one before Caiaphas the high priest, the other before Pontius Pilate the governor.

The reason of this was, that Judaea was at that time under Roman rule, forming a portion of the Roman province of Syria and administered by a Roman official, who resided in the splendid new seaport of Caesarea, fifty miles away from Jerusalem, but had also a palace in Jerusalem, which he occasionally visited.

It was not the policy of Rome to strip the countries of which she became mistress of all power. She flattered them by leaving in their hands at least the insignia of self-government, and she conceded to them as much home rule as was compatible with the retention of her paramount authority. She was specially tolerant in matters of religion. Thus the ancient ecclesiastical tribunal of the Jews, the Sanhedrim, was still allowed to try all religious questions and punish offenders. Only, if the sentence chanced to be a capital one, the case had to be re-tried by the governor, and the carrying out of the sentence, if it was confirmed, devolved upon him.

It was at the instance of the ecclesiastical authorities that Jesus was arrested, and they condemned Him to death; but they were not at liberty to carry out their sentence: they had to take Him before Pilate, who chanced at the time to be in the city, and he tried the case over again, they of course being the accusers at his bar.

Not only were there two trials, but in each trial there were three separate stages or acts. In the first, or ecclesiastical trial, Jesus had first to appear before Annas, then before Caiaphas and the Sanhedrim during the night, and again before the same body after daybreak. And in the second, or civil trial, He appeared first before Pilate, who refused to confirm the judgment of the Jews; then Pilate attempted to rid himself of the case by sending the Culprit to Herod of Galilee, who happened also to be at the time in Jerusalem; but the case came back to the Roman governor again, and, against his conscience, he confirmed the capital sentence.

But let me explain more fully what were the three acts in the ecclesiastical trial.[2]

Jesus, we are informed by St. John, was taken first to Annas. This was an old man of seventy years, who had been high priest twenty years before. As many as five of his sons succeeded him in this office, which at that period was not a life appointment, but was generally held only for a short time; and the reigning high priest at this time, Caiaphas, was his son-in-law. Annas was a man of very great consequence, the virtual head of ecclesiastical affairs, though Caiaphas was the nominal head. He had come originally from Alexandria in Egypt on the invitation of Herod the Great. He and his family were an able, ambitious and arrogant race. As their numbers multiplied, they became a sort of ruling caste, pushing themselves into all important offices. They were Sadducees, and were perfect types of that party—cold, haughty, worldly. They were intensely unpopular in the country; but they were feared as much as they were disliked. Greedy of gain, they ground the people with heavy ritual imposts. It is said that the traffic within the courts of the temple, which Jesus condemned so sternly a few days before, was carried on not only with their connivance but for their enrichment. If this was the case, the conduct of Jesus on that occasion may have profoundly incensed the high-priestly caste against Him.

Indeed, it was probably the depth of his hatred which made Annas wish to see Jesus in the hands of justice. The wary Sadducee had in all likelihood taken a leading part in the transaction with Judas and in the sending out of the troops for Christ's apprehension. He, therefore, waited out of bed to see what the upshot was to be; and those who took Jesus brought Him to Annas first. But whatever interrogation Annas may have subjected Him to was entirely informal.[3]

It allowed time, however, to get together the Sanhedrim. Messengers were dispatched to scour the city for the members at the midnight hour, because the case was urgent and could not brook delay. None knew what might happen if the multitude, when it awoke in the morning, found the popular Teacher in the hands of His unpopular enemies. But, if the trial were all over before daybreak and Jesus already in the strong hands of the Romans before the multitude had learnt that anything was going on, there would be nothing to fear. So the Sanhedrim was assembled under cloud of night; and the proceedings went forward in the small hours of the morning in the house of Caiaphas, to which Jesus had been removed.

This was not strictly legal, however, because the letter of the law did not allow this court to meet by night. On this account, although the proceedings were complete and the sentence agreed upon during the night, it was considered necessary to hold another sitting at daybreak. This was the third stage of the trial; but it was merely a brief rehearsal, for form's sake, of what had been already done.[4] Therefore, we must return to the proceedings during the night, which contain the kernel of the matter.

Imagine, then, a large room forming one side of the court of an Oriental house, from which it is separated only by a row of pillars, so that what is going on in the lighted interior is visible to those outside. The room is semicircular. Round the arc of the semicircle the half-hundred or more[5] members sit on a divan. Caiaphas, the president, occupies a kind of throne in the centre of the opposite wall. In front stands the Accused, facing him, with the jailers on the one side and the witnesses on the other.

How ought any trial to commence? Surely with a clear statement of the crime alleged and with the production of witnesses to support the charge. But, instead of beginning in this way, "the high priest asked Jesus of His disciples and of His doctrine."

The insinuation was that He was multiplying disciples for some secret design and teaching them a secret doctrine, which might be construed into a project of revolution. Jesus, still throbbing with the indignity of being arrested under cloud of night, as if He were anxious to escape, and by a force so large as to suggest that He was the head of a revolutionary band, replied, with lofty self-consciousness, "Why askest thou Me? Ask them that heard Me what I have said unto them; behold, they know what I said." Why had they arrested Him if they had yet to learn what He had said and done? They were trying to make Him out to be an underground schemer; but they, with their arrests in secrecy and their midnight trials, were themselves the sons of darkness.

Such simple and courageous speech was alien to that place, which knew only the whining of suppliants, the smooth flatteries of sycophants, and the diplomatic phrases of advocates; and a jailer, perhaps seeing the indignant blush mount into the face of the high priest, clenched his fist and struck Jesus on the mouth, asking, "Answerest Thou the high priest so?" Poor hireling! better for him that his hand had withered ere it struck that blow. Almost the same thing once happened to St. Paul in the same place, and he could not help hurling back a stinging epithet of contempt and indignation. Jesus was betrayed into no such loss of temper. But what shall be said of a tribunal, and an ecclesiastical tribunal, which could allow an untried Prisoner to be thus abused in open court by one of its minions?

The high priest had, however, been stopped on the tack which he had first tried, and was compelled to do what he ought to have begun with—to call witnesses. But this, too, turned out a pitiful failure. They had not had time to get a charge properly made out and witnesses cited; and there was no time to wait. Evidence had to be extemporized; and it was swept up apparently from the underlings and hangers on of the court. It is expressly said by St. Matthew that "they sought false witness against Jesus to put Him to death." To put Him to death was what in their hearts they were resolved upon,—they were only trying to trump up a legal pretext, and they were not scrupulous. The attempt was, however, far from successful. The witnesses could not be got to agree together or to tell a consistent story. Many were tried, but the fiasco grew more and more ridiculous.

At length two were got to agree about something they had heard from Him, out of which, it was hoped, a charge could be constructed. They had heard Him say, "I will destroy this temple that is made with hands, and within three days I will build another made without hands." It was a sentence of His early ministry, obviously of high poetic meaning, which they were reproducing as the vulgarest prose; although, even thus interpreted, it is difficult to see what they could have made of it; because, if the first half of it meant that He was to destroy the temple, the second promised to restore it again. The high priest saw too well that they were making nothing of it; and, starting up and springing forward, he demanded of Jesus, "Answerest Thou nothing? What is it which these witness against Thee?" He affected to believe that it was something of enormity that had been alleged; but it was really because he knew that nothing could be founded on it that he gave way to such unseemly excitement.

Jesus had looked on in absolute silence while the witnesses against Him were annihilating one another; nor did He now answer a word in response to the high priest's interruption. He did not need to speak: silence spoke better than the loudest words could have done. It brought home to His judges the ridiculousness and the shamefulness of their position. Even their hardened consciences began to be uneasy, as that calm Face looked down on them and their procedure with silent dignity. It was by the uneasiness which he was feeling that the high priest was made so loud and shrill.

In short, he had been beaten along this second line quite as completely as he had been along the first. But he had still a last card, and now he played it. Returning to his throne and confronting Jesus with theatrical solemnity, he said, "I adjure Thee by the living God that Thou tell us whether Thou be the Christ, the Son of God." That is to say, he put Him on oath to tell what He claimed to be; for among the Jews the oath was pronounced by the judge, not by the prisoner.

This was one of the great moments in the life of Christ. Apparently He recognised the right of the high priest to put Him on oath; or at least He saw that silence now might be construed into the withdrawal of His claims. He knew, indeed, that the question was put merely for the purpose of incriminating Him, and that to answer it meant death to Himself. But He who had silenced those by whom the title of Messiah had been thrust upon

Him, when they wished to make Him a king, now claimed the title when it was the signal for condemnation. Decidedly and solemnly He answered, "Yes, I am"; and, as if the crisis had caused within Him a great access of self-consciousness, He proceeded, "Hereafter shall ye see the Son of Man sitting on the right hand of power and coming in the clouds of heaven." [6] For the moment they were His judges, but one day He would be their Judge; it was only of His earthly life that they could dispose, but He would have to dispose of their eternal destiny.

It has often been said that Christians have claimed for Christ what He never claimed for Himself; that He never claimed to be any more than a man, but they have made Him a God. But this great statement, made upon oath, must impress every honest mind. Every effort has, indeed, been made to deplete its terms of their importance and to reduce them to the lowest possible value. It is argued, for example, that, when the high priest asked if He were "the Son of God," he meant no more than when he asked if He were "the Christ." But what is to be said of Christ's description of Himself as "sitting on the right hand of power and coming in the clouds of heaven"? Can He who is to be the Judge of men, searching their hearts to the bottom, estimating the value of their performances, and, in accordance with these estimates, fixing their eternal station and degree, be a mere man? The greatest and the wisest of men are well aware that in the history of every brother man, and even in the heart of a little child, there are secrets and mysteries which they cannot fathom. No mere man can accurately measure the character of a fellow-creature; he cannot even estimate his own.

How this great confession lifts the whole scene! We see no longer these small men and their sordid proceedings; but the Son of man bearing witness to Himself in the audience of the universe. How little we care now what the Jewish judges will say about Him! This great confession reverberates down the ages, and the heart of the world, as it hears it from His lips, says, Amen.

The high priest had achieved his end at last. As a high priest was expected to do when he heard blasphemy, he rent his clothes, and, turning to his colleagues, he said, "What need have we of witnesses? behold, now ye have heard His blasphemy." And they all assented that Jesus was guilty, and that the sentence must be death.

Sometimes good-hearted Bible-readers, in perusing these scenes, are troubled with the thought that the judges of Jesus were conscientious. Was it not their duty, when anyone came forward with Messianic pretensions, to judge whether or not his claim was just? and did they not honestly believe that Jesus was not what He professed to be? No doubt they did honestly believe so. We must ascend to a much earlier period to be able to judge their conduct accurately. It was when the claims of Jesus were first submitted to them that they went astray. He, being such as He was, could only have been welcomed and appreciated by expectant, receptive, holy minds. The ecclesiastical authorities of Judaea in that age were anything but expectant, receptive and holy. They were totally incapable of understanding Him, and saw no beauty that they should desire Him. As He often told them Himself, being such as they were, they could not believe. The fault lay not so much in what they did as in what they were. Being in the wrong path, they went forward to the end. It may be said that they walked according to their light; but the light that was in them was darkness. Their proceedings, however, on this occasion will not tend to soften the heart of anyone who looks into them carefully. They had hardly the least show of justice. There was no regular charge or regular evidence, and no thought whatever of allowing the Accused to bring counter-evidence; the same persons were both accusers and judges; the sentence was a foregone conclusion; and the entire proceedings consisted of a series of devices to force the Accused into some statement which would supply a colourable pretext for condemning Him.[7]

But it was by what ensued after the sentence of condemnation was passed that these men cut themselves off forever from the sympathy of the tolerant and generous. A court of law ought to be a place of dignity; when a great issue is tried and a solemn judgment passed, it ought to impress the judges themselves; even the condemned, when a death sentence has been passed, ought to be hedged round with a certain awe and respect. But that blow inflicted with impunity at the commencement of the trial by a minion of the court was too clear an index of the state of mind of all present. There was no solemnity or greatness of any kind in their thoughts; nothing but resentment and spite at Him who had thwarted and defied them, lessened them in the public estimation and stopped their unholy gains. A perfect sea of such feelings had long been gathering in their hearts; and now, when the opportunity came, it broke loose upon Him. They struck Him with their sticks; they spat in His face; they drew something over His head and, smiting Him again, cried, "Christ, prophesy who smote Thee." [8] One would wish to believe that it was only by the miserable underlings that such things were done; but the narrative makes it too clear that the masters led the way and the servants followed.

There are terrible things in man. There are some depths in human nature into which it is scarcely safe to look. It was by the very perfection of Christ that the uttermost evil of His enemies was brought out. There is a passage in "Paradise Lost," where a band of angels, sent out to scour Paradise in search of Satan, who is hidden in the garden, discover him in the shape of a toad "squat at the ear of Eve." Ithuriel, one of the band, touches him with his spear, whereat, surprised, he starts up in his own shape,—

> "for no falsehood can endure Touch of celestial temper, but returns Of force to its own likeness."

But the touch of perfect goodness has often the opposite effect: it transforms the angel into the toad, which is evil's own likeness.

Christ was now getting into close grips with the enemy He had come to this world to overcome; and, as it clutched Him for the final wrestle, it exhibited all its ugliness and discharged all its venom.[9] The claw of the dragon was in His flesh, and its foul breath in His mouth. We cannot conceive what such insult and dishonour must have been to His sensitive and regal mind. But He rallied His heart to endure and not to faint; for He had come to be the death of sin, and its death was to be the salvation of the world.

[1] Here would come in the curious little notice in St. Mark: "And there followed Him a certain young man, having a linen cloth cast about his naked body; and the young men laid hold on him; and he left the linen cloth and fled from them naked"; on which I have not commented, not well knowing, in truth, what to make of it. It may be designed to show the rudeness of the soldiery, and the peril in which any follower of Jesus would have been had he been caught. Some have supposed that the young man was St. Mark, and that this is the painter's signature in an obscure corner of his picture. (See Holzmann in *Handcommentar zum Neuen Testament.*) In the first volume of the *Expositor* there is a paper on the subject by Dr. Cox, but it does not throw much light on it.

[2] On the Sanhedrim and the high priests see Schürer, *The Jewish People in the Time of Christ*, div. ii., vol. i.

[3] This, many think, is what is given in St. John.

[4] Many think that this is what is given in St. Luke.

[5] The full number was seventy-one, including the president.

[6] See Psalm cx. 1, and Dan. vii. 13.

[7] Even Jost, the Jewish historian, calls it a murder; but he does not believe that there was an actual trial; and in this Edersheim agrees with him.

[8] In allusion to His claim to be the Messianic Prophet. The Roman soldiers, on the other hand, ridiculed His claim to be a King.

[9] "The central figure is the holiest Person in history, but round Him stand or strive the most opposed and contrasted moral types. . . . The men who touch Him in this supreme hour of His history do so only to have their essential character disclosed."—FAIRBAIRN.

CHAPTER III.

THE GREAT DENIAL

To the ecclesiastical trial of our Lord there is a side-piece, over which we must linger before proceeding to the civil trial. At the very hour when in the hall of the high priest's house Christ was uttering His great confession, one of His disciples was, in the court of the same building, pouring out denial after denial.

I.

When Jesus was bound in Gethsemane and led away back to Jerusalem, all His disciples forsook Him and fled. They disappeared, I suppose, among the bushes and trees of the garden and escaped into the surrounding country or wherever they thought they would be safe.

But two of the Twelve—St. Peter and St. John, who tells the story—soon rallied from the first panic and followed, at a distance,[1] the band in whose midst their Master was. Keeping in the shadow of the trees by the roadside, keeping in the shadow of the houses in the streets, they stole after the moving mass. At last, when it got near its destination—the palace of the high priest—-they hurried forward; and St. John went in with the crowd; but somehow, probably through irresolution, St. Peter was left outside in the street; and the door was shut.

To understand what follows, it is necessary to describe more in detail the construction of such a house as the high priest's palace; for it was very unlike most of our houses. A Western house looks into the street, but an Oriental into its own interior, having no opening to the front except a great arched gateway, shut with a heavy door or gate. When this door is opened, it discloses a broad passage, penetrating the front building and leading into a square, paved courtyard, open to the sky, round which the house is built, and into which its rooms, both upstairs and downstairs, look. A similar arrangement is to be seen in some large warehouses in our own cities, or you may have seen it in large hotels on the Continent. It only requires to be added that on the side of the passage, inside the outer gate, there is a room or lodge for the porter or portress, who opens and shuts the gate; and in the gate there is a little wicket by which individuals can be let in or out.

When the band conducting Jesus appeared in front of the palace, no doubt the portress opened the large gate to admit them and then shut it again. They passed under the archway into the court, which they crossed, and then entered one of the apartments overlooking the courtyard. But the police and other underlings employed in the arrest, their work being now done, stayed outside, and, as it was midnight and the weather was cold, they lighted a fire there under the open sky and, gathering round it, began to warm themselves.

As has been said, John went in through the gate with the crowd, but Peter was somehow shut out. John, who seems to have occupied a higher social position than the rest of the Twelve, was known to the high priest, and, therefore, probably was acquainted with the palace and knew the servants; and, when he noticed that Peter had been left out, he went to the portress and got her to let him in by the wicket-gate.

It was a friendly act; and yet, as the event proved, it was unintentionally an ill turn: John led Peter into temptation. The best of friends may do this sometimes to one another; for the situation into which one man may enter without peril may be dangerous to another. One man may mingle freely in company which another cannot enter without terrible risks. There are amusements in which one Christian can take part, though they would ruin another if he touched them. A mind matured and disciplined may read books which would kindle the fire of hell in a mind less experienced. There are always two things that go to the making of a temptation: there is the particular set of circumstances to be encountered on the one hand, and there is the peculiar character or history of the person entering into the situation on the other. We need to remember this if we are to defend either ourselves or others against temptation.

II.

John no doubt, as soon as he got Peter inside the door, hurried away across the court into the hall where Jesus was, to witness the proceedings.

Not so Peter. He was not familiar with the place as John was; and he had the shyness of a plain man at the sight of the inside of a great house. Besides, he was under fear of being recognized as a follower of Christ and apprehended. Now also the unlucky blow he had made at Malchus at the gate of Gethsemane had to be paid for, because it greatly increased his chance of detection.

He remained, therefore, just inside the great door, watching from the shadows of the archway what was going on inside, and, without knowing it, himself being watched by the portress from her coigne of vantage. He was ill at ease; for he did not know what to do. He did not dare to go, like John, into the judgment-hall. Perhaps he half wished he could get out into the street again. He was in a trap.

At last he strolled forward to the group round the fire and, sitting down among them, commenced to warm himself. It was a miscellaneous group there in the glare of the fire, and no notice was taken of him. He took his place as if he were one of them.

It was, however, a dangerous situation in another sense than he supposed. It was of bodily peril he was in terror; he did not anticipate danger to his soul; yet this was very near. It is always dangerous when a follower of Christ is sitting among Christ's enemies without letting it be known what he is. "Blessed is the man that walketh not in the counsel of the ungodly, nor standeth in the way of sinners, nor sitteth in the seat of the scornful." It is more than probable that when Peter sat down the air was ringing with jest and laughter about Jesus; but he did not interrupt: he kept silence and tried to look as like one of the scorners as he could. But not to confess Christ is the next step to denying Him.

Temptation, as is its wont, came suddenly and from the most unexpected quarter. As has been said, when he was skulking beneath the archway, his movements were noted by the portress. They were suspicious, and she, with a woman's cleverness, divined his secret. Accordingly, when she was relieved at her post by another maid, she not only pointed him out to this companion and communicated to her what she thought about him, but, in passing to her room, she went up to the fire among the soldiers and, looking him straight in the face, said, with a malicious twinkle in her eye, This is one of the Nazarene's followers.

Peter was taken completely by surprise. It was as if a mask had been torn from his face. In a moment the instinct of terror seized him; perhaps, too, the instinct of shame at being thought a disciple of Him they were mocking. Indeed, there was a further shame: how could he confess himself the disciple of the Master whom he had heard blasphemed without protest? He had denied his Master in act before he denied Him in word; and the preceding act made the word also necessary. "I do not know what you mean," he said, with a surly frown; and away she tripped laughing, having done her work quite successfully.

None pursued the subject. But Peter was uneasy, and took the earliest opportunity of escaping from the fireside. He went away into the archway, intending apparently, if he could, to get out of the place altogether. But here the trap was closed; for the other maid, whose attention had been directed to him, and who may have been laughing from a distance at her neighbour's sally, was standing at the door of her lodge, with two or three men; and, pointing him out to them as he came forward, she said, "That is one of the Nazarene's followers."

Poor Peter! felled to the ground a second time by the touch of a woman's hand. But how often has the saucy tongue and jeering laugh of a woman made a man ashamed of the highest and holiest! Peter flung at her an angry oath and, turning on his heel, went back again to the fire.

He was now completely panic-stricken, and lost all self-control. He was boiling with conflicting emotions and could not keep quiet. Assuming an air of defiance and indifference, he plunged into the conversation, speaking loudly to throw off suspicion, but really defeating his own object; for he drew attention on himself, and they scanned him the more narrowly the more excited he became. A relative of Malchus, whose ear he had cut off, recognised him. His loud country voice and rough Galilean accent aroused the suspicions of others. To bait such a pretender was a welcome diversion in the idle night, and soon they were all in full cry after the quarry.

Peter was thoroughly lost; like a bull in the arena attacked and stabbed on every side, he became blind with rage, terror and shame; and, pouring out denials, he added to them oaths and curses hurled at his adversaries.

The latter element was, no doubt, the resurrection of an old fisherman's habit, long since dead and buried. Peter was just the man likely to be a profane swearer in his youth—the headlong man of temper, who likes to say a thing with as much emphasis and exaggeration as possible. This is a sin whose power is generally broken instantly at conversion. While there are sins which linger on for years and require to be crucified by inches, profane swearing often dies an instantaneous death. But even in this case it is difficult to get quit of the evil past. In Peter this sin may have seemed to die at his conversion; for years it had been dead and buried; yet, when the favourable moment came, lo and behold, there it was again in vigorous life. Old habits of sin are hard to kill. We seem to have killed and buried them; but do you not sometimes hear a knocking beneath the ground? do you not feel the dead thing turning in its coffin, and see the earth moving above its grave? This is the penalty of the days given to the flesh. Till his dying day the man who has been a drunkard or a fornicator, a liar or a swearer, will have to keep watch and ward over the graveyard in which he has buried the past.

Yet there was a kind of method in the madness of Peter's profanity. When he wanted to prove that he was none of Christ's, he could not do better than take to cursing. They did not credit his assertions that he had no connection with his Master, but they could not help believing his sins. Nobody belonging to Jesus, they knew, would speak as Peter was doing. It is one of the strongest testimonies to Jesus still, that even those who do not believe in Him expect cleanness of speech and of conduct from His followers, and are astonished if those who bear His name do things which when done by others are matters of course.

IV.

While Peter was in the midst of this outbreak of denial and profanity, suddenly he saw the eyes of his tormentors turned away from him to another object.[2] It was Jesus, whom His enemies had condemned in the neighbouring judgment-hall, and whom they were now leading, amidst blows and reproaches, across the courtyard to the guard-room, where He was to be kept for two or three hours till a subsequent stage of His trial came on. As Jesus stepped down out of the hall into the courtyard, His ear had caught the accents of His disciple, and, stung with unutterable anguish, He turned quickly round in the direction whence the sounds proceeded. At the same moment Peter turned, and they looked one another full in the face. Jesus did not speak; for a single syllable, even of surprise, would have betrayed His disciple. Nor could He linger; for the soldiers were hurrying Him on. But for a single instant their eyes met, and soul looked into soul. Who shall say what was in that look of Christ?[3] There may be a world in a look. It may be more eloquent than a whole volume of words. It may reveal far more than the lips can ever utter. One soul may give itself away to another in a look. A look may beatify or plunge in the depths of despair.

The look of Jesus was a talisman dissolving the spell in which Peter was held. Sin is always a kind of temporary madness; and it was manifestly so in this case. Peter was so bewildered with terror, anger and excitement that he did not know what he was doing. But the look of Jesus brought him to himself, and immediately he acted like a man. He made at once for the exit with impetuous speed.[4] And now nothing stood in his way: he got past the maid and her companions without trouble. For, indeed, the trap of temptation is only an illusion. To a resolute man it presents no obstacles.

But further, the look of Christ was a mirror in which Peter saw himself. He saw what Christ thought of him. The past came rushing back. He was the man who, in a great and never-to-be-forgotten moment, had confessed Christ and earned His hearty recognition. He was the man who, a few hours ago, had vowed, above all the rest, that he never would deny his Master. And now he had deserted Him and wounded Him to the heart in His utmost need. He had placed himself among His enemies as one of themselves and, with oaths and curses, trodden His sacred name beneath his feet. He had put off the disciple and reverted to the rudeness of his godless youth. He was a perjured traitor. All this was in that look of Christ.

But there was far more in it. It was a rescuing look. If any friend had met Peter rushing out from the scene of his sin, he might well have been terrified for what might happen. Where was he rushing to? Was it to the precipice over which Judas plunged not many hours afterwards? Peter was not very far from that. Had it been an angry look he saw on Christ's face when their eyes met, this might have been his fate. But there was not a spark of anger in it. There was pain, no doubt, and there was immeasurable disappointment. But deeper than these—rising up from below them and submerging them—there was the Saviour's instinct, that instinct which made Him reach out His hand

and grasp Peter when he was sinking in the sea. With this same instinct He grasped Him now.

In that look of an instant Peter saw forgiveness and unutterable love. If he saw himself in it, he saw still more his Saviour—such a revelation of the heart of Christ as he had never yet known. He saw now what kind of Master he had denied; and it broke his heart. It is this that always breaks the heart. It is not our sin that makes us weep; it is when we see what kind of Saviour we have sinned against. He wept bitterly; not to wash out his sin, but because even already he knew it had been washed out. The former weeping is a pelting shower; this is the close, prolonged downpour, which penetrates deep and fertilises the plants of the soul at their very roots.

Indeed, this was the real beginning of all the good St. Peter was to do in the world. But we will not speak of this now. Let our last thought be of Him who, in the crisis and extremity of His own suffering, when He heard His name not only denied but mingled with oaths and curses, yielded not one moment to the resentment which such an act of treachery might have occasioned, but, forgetting His own sorrows and overmastered with the instincts of the Saviour, threw into a look such a world of kindness and of love that, in an instant, it lifted the falling disciple from the gulf and set him on the rock where he ever afterwards stood, himself a rock in the constancy of his faith and the vigor of his testimony.

[1] *makrothen* .

[2] It is to St. Luke we owe the account here given of Peter's awakening; but he also refers to the crowing of the cock, the only cause mentioned by the other Evangelists. There is no difficulty in understanding that such a psychological crisis may have been due to two lines of suggestion.

[3] Mrs. Browning's sonnets on this subject must be quoted in full:

"Two sayings of the Holy Scriptures beat
Like pulses in the Church's brow and breast;
And by them we find rest in our unrest,
And, heart-deep in salt tears, do yet entreat
God's fellowship, as if on heavenly seat.
The first is JESUS WEPT; whereon is prest
Full many a sobbing face, that drops its best
And sweetest waters on the record sweet.
And one is where the Christ, denied and scorned,
LOOKED UPON PETER. Oh to render plain,
By help of having loved a little and mourned,
That look of sovran love and sovran pain,

Which He, who could not sin yet suffered, turned
On him who could reject but not sustain.

"The Saviour looked on Peter. Ay, no word,
No gesture of reproach; the heavens serene,
Though heavy with armed justice, did not lean
Their thunders that way; the forsaken Lord
Looked only on the traitor. None record
What that look was; none guess; for those who have seen
Wronged lovers loving through a death-pang keen,
Or pale-cheeked martyrs smiling to a sword,
Have missed Jehovah at the judgment call.
And Peter from the height of blasphemy—
'I never knew this man'—did quail and fall,
As knowing straight THAT GOD; and turnèd free,
And went out speechless from the face of all,
And filled the silence, weeping bitterly.

I think: that look of Christ might seem to say:
'Thou, Peter! art thou a common stone
Which I at last must break My heart upon,
For all God's charge to His high angels may
Guard My feet better? Did I yesterday
Wash *thy* feet, My beloved, that they should run
Quick to destroy me 'neath the morning sun?
And do thy kisses, like the rest, betray?
The cock crows coldly. Go, and manifest
A late contrition, but no bootless fear!
For, when thy final need is dreariest,
Thou shall not be denied, as I am here;
My voice to God and angels shall attest,
Because I KNOW this man, let him be clear.'"

[4] This may be the meaning of *epibalon*; but it is much disputed. Other interpretations are: (1) = *epeballe klaiein*, he began to weep; (2) with head covered—in mourning.

CHAPTER IV.

THE CIVIL TRIAL

In the chapter before last we saw the Sanhedrim pass a death sentence on Jesus. Gladly would they have carried it out in the Jewish fashion—by stoning. But, as was then explained, it was not in their power: their Roman masters, while conceding to the native courts the power of trying and punishing minor offences, reserved to themselves the prerogative of life and death; and a case in which a capital sentence had been passed in a Jewish court had to go before the representative of Rome in the country, who tried it over again, and might either confirm or reverse the sentence. Accordingly, after passing sentence on Jesus themselves, the Sanhedrists had to lead Him away to the tribunal of the governor.

I.

The representative of Imperial Rome in Palestine at this time was Pontius Pilate. The position which he held may perhaps be best realised by thinking of one of our own subordinate governors in India; with the difference, however, that it was a heathen, not a Christian power, that Pilate represented, and that it was the spirit of ancient Rome, not that of modern England, which inspired his administration. Of this spirit—the spirit of worldliness, diplomacy and expediency—he was a typical exponent; and we shall see how true to it he proved on this momentous day.[1]

Pilate had occupied his position for a good many years; yet he neither liked his subjects nor they him. The Jews were among the most intractable and difficult of all the states which the officials of Rome had to manage. Mindful of the glory of their ancient history, and still cherishing the hope of universal empire, they were impatient of the yoke of subordination; they were constantly discovering in the conduct of their rulers insults directed against their dignity or their religion; they complained of the heavy taxation and pestered their rulers with petitions. Pilate had not got on at all well with them. Between him and them there was no sympathy. He hated their fanaticism. In his quarrels with them, which were frequent, he had freely shed their blood. They accused him of corruption, cruelty, robbery, and maladministration of every description.

The residence of the governor was not in Jerusalem, in which no one accustomed to the pleasures of Rome—its theatres, baths, games, literature and society—could desire to live, but in the new coast city of Caesarea, which in its splendour and luxury was a sort of small imitation of Rome. Occasionally, however, the governor had to visit the capital for business reasons; and usually as on this occasion, he did so at the time of the Passover.

When there, he took up his residence in what had formerly been the royal palace while Judaea still had a king. It had been built by Herod the Great, who had a passion for architecture; and it was situated on the hill to the south-west of the one on which the temple stood. It was a splendid building,[2] rivalling the temple itself in appearance, and so large as to be capable of containing a small army. It consisted of two colossal wings, springing forward on either side, and a connecting building between. In front of the latter stretched a broad pavement; and here, in the open air, on a raised platform, was the scene of the trial; because the Jewish authorities would not enter the building, which to them was unclean. Pilate had to yield to their scruples, though probably cursing them in his heart. But, indeed, it was quite common for the Romans to hold courts of justice in the open air. The front of the palace, all round, was supported by massive pillars, forming broad, shady colonnades; and round the building there extended a park, with walks, trees and ponds, where fountains cast their sparkling jets high into the sunshine and flocks of tame doves plumed their feathers at the water's edge.

Through the huge gateway, then, of this palatial residence, the Jewish authorities, with their Prisoner in their midst, came pouring in the early morning. Pilate came out to receive them and seated himself on his chair of state, with his secretaries beside him, and behind him, no doubt, numbers of bronzed Roman soldiers with their stolid looks and upright spears. The Accused would have to ascend the platform, too; and over against Him stood His accusers, with Caiaphas at their head.

What a spectacle was that! The heads of the Jewish nation leading their own Messiah in chains to deliver Him up to a Gentile governor, with the petition that He should be put to death! Shades of the heroes and the prophets, who loved this nation and boasted of it and foretold its glorious fate, the hour of destiny has come, and this is the result!

It was an act of national suicide. But was it not more? Was it not the frustration of the purpose and the promise of God? So it certainly appeared to be. Yet He is not mocked. Even through human sin His purpose holds on its way. The Jews brought the Son of God to Pilate's judgment-seat, that both Jew and Gentile might unite in condemning Him; for it was part of the work of the Redeemer to expose human sin, and here was to be exhibited the *ne plus ultra* of wickedness, as the hand of humanity was lifted up against its Maker. And yet that death was to be the life of humanity; and Jesus, standing between Jew and Gentile, was to unite them in the fellowship of a common salvation. "Oh the depth both of the wisdom and knowledge of God! How unsearchable are His judgments, and His ways past finding out!"

II.

Pilate at once demanded what was the accusation which they brought against the Prisoner.

The reply was a characteristic one, "If He were not a malefactor, we would not have delivered Him up unto thee." This was as broad a hint as they could give that they desired the governor to waive his right to re-try the case, accepting their trial of it as sufficient, and content himself with the other half of his prerogative—the passing and the execution of the sentence. Sometimes provincial governors did so, either through indolence or out of compliment to the native authorities; and especially in a religious cause, which a foreigner could not be expected to understand, such a compliment might seem a boon which it was not unreasonable to ask.

But Pilate was not in a yielding mood, and retorted, "Take ye Him and judge Him according to your law." This was as much as to say: If I am not to hear the case, then I will neither pass the sentence nor inflict the punishment; if you insist on this being a case for yourselves as ecclesiastics, then keep it to yourselves; but, if you do, you must be content with such a punishment as the law permits you to inflict.

To them this was gall and wormwood, because it was for the life of Christ they were thirsting, and they well knew that imprisonment or beating with rods was as far as they could go. The cold, keen Roman, as proud as themselves, was making them feel the pressure of Rome's foot on their neck, and he enjoyed a malicious pleasure in extorting from them the complaint, "It is not lawful for us to put any man to death."

Forced against their will and their expectation to formulate a charge, they began to pour forth many vehement accusations; out of which at length three emerged with some distinctness—first, that He was perverting the nation; second, that He forbade to pay the imperial tribute; and third, that He set Himself up as a king.

It will be observed that they never mentioned the charge on which they had condemned Him themselves. It was for none of these three things that they had condemned Him, but for blasphemy. They knew too well, however, that if they advanced such a charge in this place, the likelihood was that it would be sneered out of court. It will be remembered how a Roman governor, mentioned in the life of St. Paul, dealt with such a charge: "Gallio said unto the Jews, If it were a matter of wrong or wicked lewdness, O ye Jews, reason would that I should bear with you; but, if it be a question of words and names, and of your law, look ye to it; for I will be no judge of such matters. And he drave them from the judgment-seat." [3] And, although of course Pilate could not have dared to exhibit the same cynical disdain for what he would have called Jewish superstition, yet they knew that it was in his heart.

But their inability to bring forward the real charge put them in a false position, the dangers of which they did not escape. They had to extemporise crimes, and they were not scrupulous about it.

Their first charge—that Jesus was perverting the nation[4]—was vague. But what are we to say of the second—that He forbade to pay the imperial tribute? When we remember His reply that very week to the question whether or not it was lawful to pay tribute—"Render unto Caesar the things which are Caesar's, and unto God the things which are God's"—it looks very like a deliberate falsehood.[5] There was more colour in their third statement—that He said He was Christ a King—for He had at their tribunal solemnly avowed Himself to be the Christ. Yet, in this case, also, they were well aware that to the ear of a Roman the claim that He was a king would convey a different meaning from that conveyed to their ears by the claim to be the Christ. Indeed, at bottom their objection to Him was just that He did not sufficiently claim to be a king in the Roman sense. They were eagerly looking for a king, of splendour and military renown, to break the Roman yoke and make Jerusalem the capital of a worldwide empire; and it was because the spirit and aims of Jesus were alien to such ambitions that they despised and hated Him.

Pilate understood perfectly well with whom he was dealing. He could only be amused with their zeal for the payment of the Roman tribute. One of the Evangelists says, "He knew that for envy they had delivered Him." How far he was already acquainted with the career of Jesus we cannot tell. He had been governor all the time of the movement inaugurated by the Baptist and continued by Christ, and he can hardly have remained in entire ignorance of it. The dream of his wife, which we shall come to soon, seems to prove that Jesus had already been a theme of conversation in the palace; and perhaps the tedium of a visit to Jerusalem may have been relieved for the governor and his wife by the story of the young Enthusiast who was bearding the fanatic priests. Pilate displays, all through, a real interest in Jesus and a genuine respect. This was no doubt chiefly due to what he himself saw of His bearing at his tribunal; but it may also have been partly due to what he had already heard about Him. At all events there is no indication that he took the charges against Jesus seriously. The two first he seems never to have noticed; but the third—that He was setting Himself up as a king, who might be a rival to the emperor—was not such as he could altogether pass by.

III.

Pilate, having heard the accusations, took Jesus inside the palace to investigate them. This he did, no doubt, for the purpose of getting rid of the importunity of His accusers, which was extreme. And Jesus made no scruple, as they had done, about entering the palace. Shall we say that the Jews had rejected Him, and He was turning to the Gentiles—that the wall of partition had now fallen, and that He was trampling over its ruins?

In the silence, then, of this interior hall He and Pilate stood face to face—He in the prisoner's lonely place, Pilate in the place of power. Yet how strangely, as we now look back at the scene, are the places reversed! It is Pilate who is going to be tried—Pilate and Rome, which he represented. All that morning Pilate was being judged and exposed; and ever since he has stood in the pillory of history with the centuries gazing at him.[6] In the old pictures of the Child Christ by the great masters a halo proceeds from the Babe that lights up the surrounding figures, sometimes with dazzling effect. And it is true that on all who approached Christ, when He was in the world, there fell a light in which both the good and the evil in them were revealed. It was a search-light, that penetrated into every corner and exposed every wrinkle. Men were judged as they came near Him. Is it not so still? We never show so entirely what is in us as by the way in which we are affected by Christ. We are judging ourselves and passing sentence on ourselves for eternity by the way in which we deal with Him.

Pilate asked Him, "Art Thou the King of the Jews?" referring to the third charge brought against Him. The reply of Jesus was cautious; it was another question: "Sayest thou this of thyself, or did others tell it thee of Me?" He desired to learn in what sense the question was asked—whether from the standpoint of a Roman or from that of the Jews; because of course His answer would be different according as He was asked whether He was a king as a Roman would understand the word or according as it was understood by the Jews.

But this answer nettled Pilate, perhaps because it assumed that he might have more interest in the case than he cared to confess; and he said angrily, "Am I a Jew? Thine own nation and the chief priests have delivered Thee unto me." If he intended this to sting, the blow did not fail of its mark. Ah, tingling shame and poignant pain! His own nation—His own beloved nation, to which He had devoted His life—had given Him up to the Gentile. He felt a shame for it before the foreigner such as a slave on the block may feel before her purchaser for the father and the family that have sold her into disgrace.

Jesus at once proceeded, however, to answer Pilate's question on both sides, both on the Roman political and then on the Jewish religious side.

First, He answered negatively, "My kingdom is not of this world!" He was no rival of the Roman emperor. If He had been, the first thing He must have done would have been to assemble soldiers about Him for the purpose of freeing the country from the Roman occupation, and the very first duty of these soldiers would have been to defend the person of their king; but it could be proved that at His arrest there had been no fighting on His behalf, and that He had ordered the one follower who had drawn a sword to sheathe it again. It was not a kingdom of force and arms and worldly glory He had in view.

Yet, even in making this denial, Jesus had used the words, "My kingdom." And Pilate broke in, "Art Thou a king then?" "Yes," replied Jesus; "to this end was I born, and for this cause came I into the world, that I should bear witness unto the truth." This was His kingdom—the realm of Truth. It differs widely from that of Caesar. Caesar's empire is over the bodies of men; this is over their hearts. The strength of Caesar's empire is in soldiers, arms, citadels and navies; the strength of this kingdom is in principles, sentiments, ideas. The benefit secured by Caesar to the citizens is external security for their persons and properties; the blessings of Christ's kingdom are peace of conscience and joy in the Holy Ghost. The empire of Caesar, vast as it was, yet was circumscribed; the kingdom of Christ is without limits, and is destined to be established in every land. Caesar's empire, like every other earthly kingdom, had its day and passed out of existence; but the kingdom of Truth shall last for evermore.

It has been remarked that there was something Western rather than Oriental in this sublime saying of Christ. What a noble-minded Jew longed for above all things was righteousness; but what a noble-minded Gentile aspired after was truth. There were some spirits, in that age, even among the heathen, in whom the mention of a kingdom of truth or wisdom would have struck a responsive chord. Jesus was feeling to see whether there was in this man's soul any such longing.

He approached still nearer him when He added the searching remark, "Every one that is of the truth heareth My voice;" for it was a hint that, if he loved the truth, he must believe in Him. Jesus preached to His judge. Just as the prisoner Paul made Felix the judge tremble, and Agrippa the judge cry out, "Almost thou persuadest me to be a Christian," so Jesus, with the instinct of the preacher and the Saviour, was feeling for Pilate's conscience. He who fishes for the souls of men must use many angles; and on this occasion Jesus selected a rare one.

There will always be some who, though common appeals do not touch them, yet respond to this delicate appeal. Is truth a magic word to you? do you thirst for wisdom? There are those to whom the prizes which the majority strive for are as dross. The race for wealth, the pride of life, the distinctions of society—you laugh at them and pity them. But a golden page of a favourite poet, a thought newly minted in the glowing heat of a true thinker's mind, a pregnant word that sets your fancy ranging through eternity, a luminous doctrine that rises on the intellectual horizon like a star,—these are your wealth. You feel keenly the darkness of the world, and are perplexed by a hundred problems. Child and lover of wisdom, do you know the King of Truth? This is He who can satisfy your craving for light and lead you out of the maze of speculation and error.

But is it true, as He says here, that everyone who is of the truth heareth His voice? Is not the world at present full of men and women who are in search of truth, yet pass Christ by? It is a very strong word He uses; it is, "every one who has been born of the truth." Have you actually clambered on Truth's knees, and clung to her neck, and fed at her breast? There are many who seek truth earnestly with the intellect, but do not desire it to rule their conduct or purify their heart. But only those who seek truth with their whole being are her true children; and to these the voice of Christ, when it is discerned, is like the sunrise to the statue of Memnon or as the call of spring to the responsive earth.

Alas! Pilate was no such man. He was incapable of spiritual aspiration; he was of the earth earthy; he sought for nothing which the eye cannot see or the hand handle. To him a kingdom of truth and a king of truth were objects of fairyland or castles in the air. "What is truth?" he asked; but, as he asked, he turned on his heel, and did not wait for an answer. He asked only as a libertine might ask, What is virtue? or a tyrant, What is freedom?

But he was clearly convinced that Jesus was innocent. He judged Him to be an amiable enthusiast, from whom Rome had nothing to fear. So he went out and pronounced His acquittal: "I find in Him no fault at all."

[1] On Pilate there is an essay of extraordinary subtlety and power in Candlish's *Scripture Characters*.

[2] An eloquent account in Keim (vi., p. 80, English tr.), who gives the authorities: "in part a tyrant's stronghold, and in part a fairy pleasure-house."

[3] Acts xviii. 14-16.

[4] *ethnos*, not *laos*: they were speaking to a heathen.

[5] Keim calls it "a very flagrant lie."

[6] "Socrates, quum omnium sapientissime sanctissimeque vixisset, ita in judicio capitis pro se dixit, ut non supplex aut reus, sed magister aut dominus videretur judicum."—CICERO.

CHAPTER V.

JESUS AND HEROD

Pilate had tried Jesus and found Him innocent; and so he frankly told the members of the Sanhedrim, thereby reversing their sentence. What ought to have followed? Of course Jesus ought to have been released and, if necessary, protected from the feeling of the Jews.

Why was this not what happened? An incident in the life of Pilate, narrated by a secular historian, may best explain. Some years before the trial of Jesus, Pilate, newly settled in the position of governor of Judaea, resolved to remove the headquarters of the Roman army from Caesarea to Jerusalem; and the soldiers entered the Holy City with their standards, each of which bore the image of the emperor. To the Jewish mind these images were idolatrous, and their presence in Jerusalem was looked upon as a gross insult and desecration. The foremost men of the city poured down to Caesarea, where Pilate was staying, and besought him to remove them. He refused, and for five days the discussion went on. At length he was so irritated that he ordered them to be surrounded by soldiers, and threatened to have them put to death unless they became silent and dispersed. They, however, in no way dismayed, threw themselves on the ground and laid bare their necks, crying that they would rather die than have their city defiled. And the upshot was that Pilate had to yield, and the army was withdrawn from Jerusalem.[1]

Such was the governor, and such were the people with whom he had to deal. He was no match for them, when their hearts were set on anything and their religious prejudices roused. In the present case they did with him exactly as they had done on that early occasion. He declared Jesus innocent, and thereupon the trial ought to have been at an end. But they raised an angry clamour—"they were the more fierce," says St. Luke—and began to pour out new accusations against the Prisoner.

Pilate had not nerve enough to resist. He weakly turned to Jesus Himself, asking, "Hearest Thou not what these witness against Thee?" But Jesus "answered to him never a word." He would not, by a single syllable, give sanction to any prolongation of the proceedings: "insomuch that the governor marvelled greatly." Flustered and irresolute himself, he could not comprehend this majestic composure. The stake of Jesus in the proceedings was nothing less than His life; yet He was the only calm person in the whole assemblage.

Suddenly, however, amidst the confusion a way of escape from his embarrassing situation seemed to open to Pilate. They were crying, "He stirreth up the people, teaching throughout all Jewry, beginning from Galilee to this place." The mention of Galilee was intended to excite prejudice against Jesus, because Galilee was noted as a hotbed of insurrection. But it set agoing a different train of thought in the mind of Pilate, who asked anxiously if He was a Galilean. It had flashed upon him that Herod, the ruler of Galilee, was in the city at the time, having come for the Passover celebration; and, as it was not an unusual procedure in Roman law to transfer a prisoner from the territory where he had been arrested to his place of origin or of domicile, it seemed to him a happy inspiration to send Jesus to be tried by the ruler of the province to which He belonged, and so get rid altogether of the case.[2] He acted at once on this idea; and, under the escort of Pilate's soldiers, Jesus and His accusers were sent away to the ancient palace of the Maccabees, in which Herod used to reside on his visits to the Holy City.

Thus was Jesus, on this day of shame, tossed, like a ball, from hand to hand— from Annas to Caiaphas, from Caiaphas to Pilate, from Pilate to Herod, with more to follow; and these weary marches[3] in chains and in the custody of the officers of justice, with His persecutors about Him, are not to be forgotten in the catalogue of His sufferings.

I.

There are several Herods mentioned in the New Testament, and it must be made clear which of them this was.

The first of them was he who slew the babes of Bethlehem, when the infant Saviour was carried away to Egypt. He was called Herod the Great, and reigned over the whole country, though only by permission of the Romans. At his death his dominions were divided among his sons by the foreigner, who thus more effectually brought the country under control; for the smaller the size of subject states the more absolute is the power of the suzerain. Judaea was given to Archelaus; but it was soon taken from him, to be administered by the Romans themselves through their procurators, of whom Pilate was one. Galilee and Peraea were given to another son, Antipas; and a region more to the north to a third, Philip. Our present Herod is Antipas.

He was a man of some ability and at the outset of his career gave promise of ruling well. Like his father, he had a passion for architecture, and among his achievements in this line was the building of the city of Tiberias, well known in connection with modern missions. But he took a step which proved fatal when he entered into an intrigue with Herodias, the wife of his own brother Philip. She left her husband to come to him, and he sent away his own wife, the daughter of Aretas, the king of Arabia Petraea. Herodias was a much stronger character than he; and she remained at his side through life as his evil genius. Better aspirations were not, however, wholly extinguished in him even by this fall. When the Baptist began to fire the country, he took an interest in his preaching, and invited him to the palace, where he heard him gladly, till John said, "It is not lawful for thee to have her." For this the great preacher was cast into prison; but even then Herod frequently sent for him. Manifestly he was under religious impression. He admired the character and the teaching of John. It is said "he did many things." Only he could not and would not do the one thing needful: Herodias still retained her place. Naturally she feared and hated the man of God, who was seeking to remove her; and she plotted against him with implacable malignity. She was only too successful, making use of her own daughter—not Antipas', but her first husband's—for her purpose. On the king's birthday Salome danced before Herod and so intoxicated him with her skill and beauty, that, heated and overcome, he promised—the promise showing the man—to give her whatever she might ask, even to the half of his kingdom; and when the young witch, well drilled by her mother in the craft of hell, asked the head of the man of God, she was not refused.

This awful crime filled his subjects with horror, and when, soon afterwards, King Aretas, the father of his discarded wife, invaded the country, to revenge his daughter's wrong, and inflicted on him an ignominious defeat, this reverse was popularly regarded as a divine punishment for what he had done. His own mind was haunted by the spectres of remorse, as we learn from the fact that, when he heard of the preaching of Jesus, his first thought was that this was John the Baptist risen from the dead. Indeed, from this point he seems to have rapidly deteriorated. Feeling the aversion of the minds of his subjects, he turned more and more to foreign customs. His court became distinguished for Roman imitations and affectations. The purveyors of pleasure, who in that age hawked their wares from one petty court to another—singers, dancers, jugglers and the like—were welcome at Tiberias. The fibre of his character was more and more relaxed, till it became a mere mass of pulp, ready to receive every impression but able to retain none. His annual visits to Jerusalem even, at Passover time, were inspired less by devotion than by the hope of amusement. In so large a concourse there would at any rate be acquaintances to see and news to hear; and who could tell what excitement might turn up?

II.

His reception of Jesus was thoroughly characteristic. Had he had the conscience even of a bad man, he might have been abashed to see the Baptist's Friend. Once he had been moved with terror at the mere rumour of Jesus; but that was all past; these emotions had been wiped out by newer ones and forgotten. He was "exceeding glad" to see Him. First, it was an excitement; and this was something for such a man. Then, it was a compliment from the Roman; indeed, we are told that Pilate and he had aforetime been at enmity, but by this attention were made friends again. His delight, however, arose chiefly from the hope that he might see Jesus working a miracle. For two or three years his own dominions had been ringing with the fame of the Miracle-worker, but Herod had never seen Him. Now was his chance; and no doubt entered his mind that Jesus would gratify his curiosity, or could count it anything but an honour to get the opportunity of displaying His skill.

Such was Herod's estimate of Christ. He put Him on the level of a new dancer or singer; he looked on His miracles as a species of conjuring or magic; and he expected from Him the same entertainment as he might have obtained from any wandering professor of magical arts.

At once he addressed Him in the friendliest manner and questioned Him in many words. Apparently he quite forgot the purpose for which Pilate had sent Him. He did not even wait for any replies, but went rambling on. He had thought much about religion, and he wished Jesus to know it. He had theories to ventilate, puzzles to propound, remarks to make. A man who has no religion may yet have a great deal to say about religion; and there are people who like far better to hear themselves talking than to listen to any speaker, however wise. No mouth is more voluble than that of a characterless man of feeling.

III.

Herod at last exhausted himself, and then he waited for Christ to speak. But Jesus uttered not a word. The silence lasted till the pause grew awkward and painful, and till Herod grew red and angry; but Jesus would not break it with a single syllable.

For one thing, the entire proceedings were irrelevant. Jesus had been sent to Herod to be tried; but this had never been touched upon. Had Jesus, indeed, desired to deliver Himself at all hazards, this was a rare opportunity; because, if He had yielded to Herod's wishes and wrought a miracle for his gratification, no doubt He would have been acquitted and sent back loaded with gifts. But we cannot believe that such an expedient was even a temptation to Him. Never had He wrought a miracle for His own behoof, and it is inconceivable that He should have stooped to offer any justification of the estimate of Himself which this man had formed. Jesus was Herod's subject; but it was impossible for Him to look upon him with respect. How could He help feeling disdain for one who thought of Himself so basely and treated this great crisis so frivolously? To one who knew Herod's history, how loathsome must it have been to hear religious talk from his lips! There was no manliness or earnestness in the man. Religion was a mere diversion to him.

To such Christ will always be silent. Herod is the representative of those for whom there is no seriousness in life, but who live only for pleasure. There are many such. Not only has religion, in any high and serious sense, no attraction for them, but they dislike everything like deep thought or earnest work in any sphere. As soon as they are released from the claims of business, they rush off to be excited and amused; and the one thing they dread is solitude, in which they might have to face themselves. In certain classes of society, where work is not necessary to obtain a livelihood, this spirit is the predominant one: life is all a scene of gaiety; one amusement follows another; and the utmost care is taken to avoid any intervals where reflection might come in.

Religion itself may be dragged into this circle of dissipation. It is possible to go to church with substantially the same object with which one goes to a place of amusement—in the hope of being excited, of having the feelings stirred and the aesthetic sense gratified or, at the least, consuming an hour which might otherwise lie heavy on the hands. With shame be it said, there are churches enough and preachers enough ready to meet this state of mind half-way. With the fireworks of rhetoric or the witchery of music or the pomp of ritual the performance is seasoned up to the due pitch; and the audience depart with precisely the same kind of feeling with which they might leave a concert or a theatre. Very likely it is accounted a great success; but Christ has not spoken: He is resolutely mute to those who follow religion in this spirit.

Sometimes the same spirit takes another direction; it becomes speculative and sceptical and, like Herod, "questions in many words." When I have heard some people propounding religious difficulties, the answer which has risen to my lips has been, Why should you be able to believe in Christ? what have you ever done to render yourselves worthy of such a privilege? you are thinking of faith as a compliment to be paid to Christ; in reality the power to believe in Him and His words is a great privilege and honour, that requires to be purchased with thought, humility and self-denial.

We do not owe an answer to the religious objections of everyone. Religion is, indeed, a subject on which everyone takes the liberty of speaking; the most unholy and evil-living talk and write of it nothing doubting; but in reality it is a subject on which very few are entitled to be heard. We may know beforehand, from their lives, what the opinions of many must be about it; and we know what their opinions are worth.

It may be thought that Jesus ought to have spoken to Herod—that He missed an opportunity. Ought He not to have appealed to his conscience and attempted to rouse him to a sense of his sin? To this I answer that His silence was itself this appeal. Had there been a spark of conscience left in Herod, those Eyes looking him through and through, and that divine dignity measuring and weighing him, would have caused his sins to rise up out of the grave and overwhelm him. Jesus was silent, that the voice of the dead Baptist might be heard.

If we understood it, the silence of Christ is the most eloquent of all appeals. Can you remember when you used to hear Him—when the words of the Book and the preacher used to move you in church, when the singing awoke aspiration, when the Sabbath was holy ground, when the Spirit of God strove with you? And is that all passed of passing away? Does Christ speak no more? If a man is lying ill, and perceives day by day everything about him becoming silent—his wife avoiding speech, visitors sinking their voices to a whisper, footsteps falling and doors shutting noiselessly—he knows that his illness is becoming critical. When the traveller, battling with the snow-storm, sinks down at last to rest, he feels cold and painful and miserable; but, if there steals over him a soft, sweet sense of slumber and silence, then is the moment to rouse himself and fight off his peace, if he is ever to stir again. There is such a spiritual insensibility. It means that the Spirit is ceasing to strive, and Christ to call. If it is creeping over you, it is time to be anxious; for it is for your life.

IV.

How far Herod understood the silence of Jesus we cannot tell. It is too likely that he did not wish to understand. At all events he acted as if he did not; he treated it as if it were stupidity. He thought that the reason why Jesus would not work a miracle was because He could not: a pretender's powers generally forsake him when he falls into the hands of the police. Jesus, he thought, was discredited; His Messianic claims were exploded; even His followers must now be disillusioned.

So he thought and so he said; and the satellites round his throne chimed in; for there is no place where a great man's word is echoed with more parrot-like precision than in a petty court. And no doubt they considered it a great stroke of wit, well worthy of applause, when Herod, before sending Him back to Pilate, cast over His shoulders a gorgeous robe—probably in imitation of the white robe worn at Rome by candidates for office. The suggestion was that Jesus was a candidate for the throne of the country, but one so ridiculous that it would be a mistake to treat Him with anything but contempt. Thus amidst peals of laughter was Jesus driven from the presence.

[1] Josephus, "Ant.," XVIII., 3, 1.

[2] It may be questioned whether it was for trial he sent Jesus to Herod or only for advice, as Festus caused St. Paul's case to be heard by Agrippa.

[3] Called "die Gänge des Dulders," in German devotional literature.

CHAPTER VI.

BACK TO PILATE

The sending of Jesus to Herod had not, as Pilate had hoped, finished the case, and so the Prisoner was brought back to the imperial palace.

Herod had affected to treat Jesus with disdain; but in reality, as we are now aware, he had himself been tried and exposed. And Jesus returned to do the same thing for Pilate—to make manifest what manner of spirit he was of; though Pilate had no conception that this was going to happen: he was only annoyed that a case of which he thought he had got rid was thrown on his hands again. He had reluctantly to resume it, and he carried it through to the end; but, before this point was reached, his character was revealed, down to its very foundations, in the light of Christ.

Herod's spirit was that of frivolous worldliness—the worldliness which tries to turn the whole of life into a pastime or a joke; Pilate's was that of strenuous worldliness—the worldliness which makes self its aim and subordinates everything to success. Of the two this is perhaps the more common; and, therefore, it will be both interesting and instructive to watch its self-revelation under the search-light of Christ's proximity.

I.

Pilate might perhaps have been justified in suspending the release of Jesus till after he received Him back from Herod; because, although he had himself found no fault in Him, his ignorance of Jewish laws and customs might have made him hesitate about his own judgment and wish, before absolutely settling the case, to obtain the opinion of an expert. When, however, he learned that the opinion of Herod coincided with his own, there was no further excuse for delay.

Accordingly he plainly informed the Jews[1] that he had examined the Prisoner and found no fault in Him; he had also sent Him to Herod with a like result. "Therefore," he continued. Therefore—what? "Therefore," you expect to hear, "I dismiss Him from the bar acquitted, and I will protect Him, if need be, from all violence." This would have been the only conclusion in accordance with logic and justice. Pilate's conclusion was the extraordinary one: "Therefore I will chastise Him and release Him." He would inflict the severe punishment of scourging as a sop to their rage, and then release Him as a tribute to justice.

Was a more unjust proposal ever made? Yet it was thoroughly characteristic of the man who made it as well as of the system which he represented. The spirit of imperial Rome was the spirit of compromise, manoeuvre and expediency; as the spirit of government has too often been elsewhere, not only in the State but also in the Church. Pilate had settled scores of cases on the same principle—or no principle; scores of officials were conducting their administration throughout the vast Roman empire in the same way at that very time. Only to Pilate fell the sinister distinction of putting the base system in operation in the case where its true character was exposed in the light of history.

But ought we not to believe that in all other cases, however obscure the victims, the spirit manifested by Pilate has been equally displeasing to God? In our Lord's picture of the Last Judgment one striking trait is that all are astonished at the reasons assigned for their destiny. Those on the right hand are credited with feeding Christ when He was hungry, giving Him drink when He was thirsty, and so forth; and they ask in surprise, Lord, when saw we Thee hungry and fed Thee, or thirsty and gave Thee drink? In like manner those on the left are accused of seeing Christ hungry but neglecting to feed Him, of seeing Him thirsty and refusing to give Him drink, and so forth; and they ask, Lord, when saw we Thee hungry or thirsty and ministered not to Thee? You perhaps think they say so to conceal the sins of which they are conscious? Not at all. They are really astonished: they think their identity has been mistaken and that they are about to be punished for sins they have never committed. They are only aware of having neglected a few children or old women not worth thinking about. But Christ says, Each of these stood for Me, and, when you neglected or injured them, you were doing it unto Me. Thus may all life at the last prove far more high and solemn than we now imagine. Take care how you touch your brother man; you may be touching the apple of God's eye: take care how you do an injustice even to a child; you may find out at the last that it is Christ you have been assailing.

II.

Pilate had cut himself loose from principle when he declared Jesus to be innocent and yet ordered Him to be chastised. He thought, however, that he could guide his course safely enough to the point at which he aimed. We are to see how completely he failed and at last suffered total shipwreck. Hands were stretched out towards him, as he advanced, some to save him, some to do the reverse; but the impulse of his own false beginning carried him on to the fatal issue.

The first hand stretched out to him was a loving and helpful one: it was the hand of his wife. She sent to tell him of a dream she had had about his Prisoner and to warn him to have nothing to do with "that just man."

Difficulties have been made as to how she could know about Christ; but there is no real difficulty. Probably, while Jesus was away at Herod's, Pilate had entered the palace and told his wife about the singular trial and about the impression which Jesus had made upon his mind. When he left her, she had fallen asleep and dreamed about it; for, though our version makes her say, "This night I have dreamed about Him," the literal translation is "this day"; and of course there might be many causes why a lady should fall asleep in the daytime. Her dream had been such as to fill her with a vague sense of alarm, and her message to her husband was the result.

This incident has taken a strong hold of the Christian imagination and given rise to all kinds of guesses. Tradition has handed down the name of Pilate's wife as Claudia Procula; and it is said that she was a proselyte of the Jewish religion; as high-toned heathen ladies in that age not infrequently became when circumstances brought the Old Testament into their hands. The Greek Church has gone so far as to canonise her, supposing that she became a Christian. Poets and artists have tried to reproduce her dream. Many will remember the picture of it in the Doré Gallery in London. The dreaming woman is represented standing in a balcony and looking up an ascending valley, which is crowded with figures. It is the vale of years or centuries, and the figures are the generations of the Church of Christ yet to be. Immediately in front of her is the Saviour Himself, bearing His cross; behind and around Him are His twelve apostles and the crowds of their converts; behind these the Church of the early centuries, with the great fathers, Polycarp and Tertullian, Athanasius and Gregory, Chrysostom and Augustine; further back the Church of the Middle Ages, with the majestic forms and warlike accoutrements of the Crusaders rising from its midst; behind these the Church of modern times, with its heroes; then multitudes upon multitudes that no man can number pressing forward in broadening ranks, till far aloft, in the white and shining heavens, lo, tier on tier and circle upon circle, with the angels of God hovering above them and on their flanks; and in the midst, transfigured to the brightness of a star, the cross, which in its rough reality He is bearing wearily below.

Of course these are but fancies. In the woman's anxiety that no evil should befall the Innocent we may, with greater certainty, trace the vestiges of the ancient Roman justice as it may have dwelt in the noble matrons, like Volumnia and Cornelia, whose names adorn the pristine annals of her race; while the wife's solicitude to save her husband from a deed of sin associates her with the still nobler women of all ages who have walked like guardian angels by the side of men immersed in the world and liable to be coarsened by its contact, to warn them of the higher laws and the unseen powers. We can hardly doubt that the hand of God was in this dream, or that it was outstretched to save Pilate from the doom to which he was hastening.

III.

Another hand, however, was now stretched out to him; and he grasped it eagerly, thinking it was going to save him; when it suddenly pushed him down towards the abyss. It was the hand of the mob of Jerusalem.

Up to this point the actors assembled on the stage of Christ's trial were comparatively few. It had been the express desire of the Jewish authorities to hurry the case through before the populace of the city and the crowds of Passover strangers got wind of it. The proceedings had accordingly gone forward all night; and it was still early morning. As Jesus was led through the streets to Herod and back, accompanied by so many of the principal citizens, no doubt a considerable number must have gathered. But now circumstances brought a great multitude on the scene.

It was the custom of the Roman governor, on the Passover morning, to release a prisoner to the people. As there were generally plenty of political prisoners on hand, rebels against the detested Roman yoke, but, for that very reason, favourites and heroes of the Jewish populace, this was a privilege not to be forgotten; and, while the trial of Jesus was proceeding in the open air, the mob of the city came pouring through the palace gates and up the avenue, shouting for their annual gift.

For once their demand was welcome to Pilate, for he thought he saw in it a way of escape from his own difficulty. He would offer them Jesus, who had a few days before been the hero of a popular demonstration, and as an aspirant to the Messiahship would, he imagined, be the very person they should want.

It was an utterly unjust thing to do; because, first, it was treating Jesus as if He were already a condemned man, whereas Pilate had himself a few minutes before declared Him innocent; and, secondly, it was staking the life of an innocent man on a guess, which might be mistaken, as to the fancy of the mob. No doubt, however, Pilate considered it kind, as he felt sure of the disposition of the populace; and, at all events, the chance of extricating himself was too good to lose.

The minds of the mob it turned out, however, were pre-occupied with a favourite of their own. Singularly enough his name also appears to have been Jesus: "Jesus Barabbas" is the name he bears in some of the best manuscripts of the gospel of St. Matthew.[2] He was "a notable prisoner," who had been guilty of insurrection in the city, in which blood had been spilt, and was now lying in jail with the associates whose ringleader he had been. A bandit, half robber half insurrectionary leader, is a figure which easily lays hold of the popular imagination. They hesitated, however, when Pilate proposed Jesus; and Pilate seems to have sent for the other prisoner, that they might see the two side by side; for they could not, he thought, hesitate for a moment, if they had the opportunity of observing the contrast.

But this brief interval was utilised by the Sanhedrists to persuade the multitude. It must be remembered that this was not the Galilean crowd by which Jesus had been brought in triumph into the city a few days before, but the mob of Jerusalem, with whom the ecclesiastical authorities had influence.[3] The priests and scribes, then, mingled among them and used every artifice they could think of. Probably their most effective argument was to whisper that Jesus was obviously the choice of Pilate, and therefore should not be theirs.

If Pilate actually placed the two Jesuses side by side on his platform, what a sight it was! The political desperado, stained with murder, there; the Healer and Teacher, who had gone about continually doing good, the Son of man, the Son of God, here. Now which will you have—Jesus or Barabbas? And the cry came ringing from ten thousand throats, "Barabbas!"

To Jesus what must that have meant! These were the inhabitants of Jerusalem, whom He had longed to gather as a hen gathereth her chickens under her wings; they were the hearers of His words, the subjects of His miracles, the objects of His love; and they prefer to Him a murderer and a robber.

This scene has often been alleged as the self-condemnation of democracy. *Vox populi vox Dei*, its flatterers have said; but look yonder: when the multitude has to choose between Jesus and Barabbas, it chooses Barabbas. If this be so, the scene is equally decisive against aristocracy. Did the priests, scribes and nobles behave better than the mob? It was by their advice that the mob chose.

It is poor sport, on either side, to pelt opponents with such reproaches. It is better far to learn holy fear from such a scene in reference to ourselves, to our own party and to our country. What are we to admire? Whom are we to follow? In what are we to seek salvation? Certainly there are great questions awaiting the democracy. Whom will it choose—the revolutionist or the regenerator? And to what will it trust—cleverness or character? What spirit will it adopt as its own—that of violence or that of love? Which means will it employ—those which work from without inwards, or those which work from within outwards? What end will it seek—the kingdom of meat and drink, or the kingdom which is righteousness and peace and joy in the Holy Ghost? But such questions are not for the democracy alone. All classes, all parties, every generation and every country have, from time to time, to face them. And so has the individual. Perhaps all the great choices of life ultimately resolve themselves into this one—Jesus or Barabbas?

IV.

To Pilate the choice of Barabbas must have been not only a surprise, but a staggering blow. "What then," he asked, "shall I do with Jesus?" Probably he expected the answer, Give us Him too; and there can be little doubt that he would willingly have complied with such a request. But, instead of this, there came, quick as echo, the reply, "Crucify Him!" and it was more a command than a request.

He was now made sensible that what he had considered a loophole of escape was a noose into which he had thrust his head. He might, indeed, have intimated that he had only given them the prerogative to save one of the two lives, not to take either of them away. But virtually he had put both prisoners at their disposal. In this way, at all events, the mob interpreted the situation; and he did not venture to contradict them.

He was, however, deeply moved, and he did a very unusual thing: calling for a basin of water, he washed his hands before them all and said, "I am innocent from the blood of this just Person; see ye to it." This was an impressive act; yet its impressiveness was too theatrical. He washed his hands when he ought to have exerted them. And blood does not come off so easily. He could not abnegate his responsibility and cast it upon others. Public men frequently think they can do so: they say that they bow to the force of public opinion, but wash their hands of the deed. But if their position, like Pilate's, demands that they should decide for themselves and take the consequences, the guilt of sinful action clings to them and cannot be transferred. This whole scene, indeed, is a mirror for magistrates, to show them down what dark paths they may be pushed if they resign themselves to be the mere tools of the popular will. Pilate ought to have opposed the popular will at whatever risk and refused to do the deed of which he disapproved. But such a course would have involved loss to himself; and this was the real reason for his conduct.

The populace felt their triumph, and in reply to his solemn dissociation of himself from Christ's death sent back the insulting cry, "His blood be on us and on our children." Pilate was afraid of the guilt, but they were not. Well might the heavens have blackened above them at that word, and the earth shuddered beneath their feet! Profaner cry was never uttered. But they were mad with rage and reckless of everything but victory in the contest in which they were engaged. Still, their words were not forgotten in the quarter to which they were directed; and it was not long before the curse which they had invoked descended on their city and their race. Meanwhile they gained their end: the will of Pilate was breaking down before their well-directed persistency.

[1] "On the return of Jesus from Herod, the Sanhedrists do not seem to have been present. Pilate had to call them together, presumably from the temple."—EDERSHEIM.

[2] See Keim's note. Westcott and Hort reject it. Some have further seen an impressive coincidence in the name Barabbas, interpreting it "son of the father." Jesus was by no means a rare name.

[3] Hence the contrast, common in popular preaching, between the multitude crying "Hosanna" and the same multitude crying "Crucify" is incorrect.

CHAPTER VII.

THE CROWN OF THORNS.

Pilate had failed in his attempt to save Jesus from the hands of His prosecutors, whose rage against their Victim was only intensified by the struggle in which they had engaged; and there was no course now open to him but to hand Jesus over to the executioners for, at least, the preliminary tortures of crucifixion.

It is not in accordance with modern Christian sentiment to dwell very much on the physical sufferings of Christ. Once the feeling on this subject was very different: in old writers, like the mystic Tauler, for example, every detail is enlarged upon and even exaggerated, till the page seems to reek with blood and the mind of the reader grows sick with horror. We rather incline to throw a veil over the ghastly details, or we uncover them only so far as may be necessary in order to understand the condition of His mind, in which we seek His real sufferings.

The sacred body of our Lord was exposed to many shocks and cruelties before the final and complicated horrors of the crucifixion. First, there was His agony in the garden. Then—not to speak of the chains laid on Him when He was arrested—there was the blow on the face from the servant of the high priest. After His condemnation by the ecclesiastical authorities in the middle of the night they "did spit in His face and buffeted Him;" and others smote Him with the palms of their hands, saying, "Prophesy unto us, Thou Christ. Who is he that smote Thee?" The present is, therefore, the fourth access of physical suffering which He had to endure.

First, they scourged Him. This was done by the Roman soldiers by order of their master Pilate, though the governor, in all likelihood, retired from the scene while it was being inflicted. It took place, it would appear, on the platform where the trial had been held, and in the eyes of all. The victim was stripped and stretched against a pillar, or bent over a low post, his hands being tied, so that he had no means of defending himself. The instrument of torture was a sort of knout or cat-o'-nine-tails, with bits of iron or bone attached to the ends of the thongs. Not only did the blows cut the skin and draw blood, but not infrequently the victim died in the midst of the operation. Some have supposed that Pilate, out of consideration for Jesus, may have moderated either the number or the severity of the strokes; but, on the other hand, his plan of releasing Him depended on his being able to show the Jews that He had suffered severely. The inability of Jesus to bear His own cross to the place of execution was no doubt chiefly due to the exhaustion produced by this infliction; and this is a better indication of the degree of severity than mere conjecture.

After the scourging the soldiers took Him away with them to their own quarters in the palace and called together the whole band to enjoy the spectacle. Evidently they thought that He was already condemned to be crucified; and anyone condemned to crucifixion seems, after being scourged, to have been handed over to the soldiery to be handled as they pleased, just as a hunted creature, when it is caught, is flung to the dogs. And, indeed, this comparison is only too appropriate; because, as Luther has remarked, in those days men were treated as only brutes are treated now. To us it is incomprehensible how the whole band should have been called together merely to gloat over the sufferings of a fellow-creature and to turn His pain and shame into brutal mockery. This, however, was their purpose; and they enjoyed it as schoolboys enjoy the terror of a tortured animal. It must be remembered that these were men who on the field of battle were inured to bloodshed and at Rome found their chief delight in watching the sports of the arena, where gladiators butchered one another to make a Roman holiday.

Their horseplay took the form of a mock coronation. They had caught the drift of the trial sufficiently to know that the charge against Jesus was that He pretended to be a king; and lofty pretensions on the part of one who appears to be mean and poor easily lend themselves to ridicule. Besides, in their minds there was perhaps an amused scorn at the thought of a Jew aiming at a sovereignty above that of Caesar. Foreign soldiers stationed in Palestine cannot have liked the Jews, who hated them so cordially; and this may have given an edge to their scorn of a Jewish pretender.

They treated Him as if they believed Him to be a king. A king must wear the purple. And so they got hold of an old, cast-off officer's cloak of this colour and threw it over His shoulders. Then a king must have a crown. So one of them ran out to the park in which the palace stood and pulled a few twigs from a tree or bush. These happened to be thorny; but this did not matter, it was all the better; they were plaited into the rude semblance of a crown and crushed down on His head. To complete the outfit, a king must have a sceptre. And this they found without difficulty: a reed, probably used as a walking-stick, being thrust into His right hand. Thus was the mock king dressed up. And then, as on occasions of state they had seen subjects bow the knee to the emperor, saying, "*Ave, Caesar!*" so they advanced one after another to Jesus and, bending low, said, "Hail, King of the Jews!" But, after passing with mock solemnity, each turned and, with a burst of laughter, struck Him a blow, using for this purpose the reed which He had dropped. And, though I hardly dare to repeat it, they covered His face with spittle!

What a spectacle! It might have been expected that those who were themselves poor and lowly, and therefore subject to the oppression of the powerful, would have felt sympathy and compassion for one of their own station when crushed by the foot of tyranny. But there is no cruelty like the cruelty of underlings. There is an instinct in all to wish to see others cast down beneath themselves; and, especially, if one who has aimed high is brought low, there is a sense of personal exultation at his downfall. Such are the base passions which lie at the bottom of men's hearts; and the dregs of the dregs of human nature were revealed on this occasion.

What must it have been to Jesus to look on it—to have it thrust on His sight and into contact with His very person, so that He could not get away? What must it have been to Him, with His delicate bodily organism and sensitive mind, to be in the hands of those rude and ruthless men? It was, however, necessary, in order that He might fully accomplish the work which He had come to the world to perform. He had come to redeem humanity—to go down to the very lowest depths to seek and to save the lost; and, therefore, He had to make close acquaintance with human nature in its worst specimens and its extremest degradation. He was to be the Saviour of sinners as bad and degraded as even these soldiers; and, therefore, He had to come in contact with them and see what they were.

Thus have I passed as lightly as was possible over the details; nor would my readers wish me to dwell on them further. But it will be profitable to linger on this spot a little longer, in order to learn the lessons of the scene.

First, notice in the conduct of the tormentors of Jesus the abuse of one of the gifts of God. In the conduct of the Roman soldiers from first to last the most striking feature is that at every point they turned their work into horseplay and merriment. Now, laughter is a gift of God. It is a kind of spice which the Creator has given to be taken along with the somewhat unpalatable food of ordinary life. It is a kind of sunshine to enliven the landscape, which is otherwise too dull and sombre. The power of seeing the amusing side of things immensely lightens the load of life; and he who possesses the gift of evoking hearty and innocent mirth may be a true benefactor of his species.[1]

But, while laughter is a gift of God, there is no other gift of His which is more frequently abused and converted from a blessing into a curse. When laughter is directed against sacred things and holy persons; when it is used to belittle and degrade what is great and reverend; when it is employed as a weapon with which to torture weakness and cover innocence with ridicule—then, instead of being the foam on the cup at the banquet of life, it becomes a deadly poison. Laughter guided these soldiers in their inhuman acts; it concealed from them the true nature of what they were doing; and it wounded Christ more deeply than even the scourge of Pilate.

A second thing to be noticed is that it was against the kingly office of the Redeemer that the opposition of men was directed on this occasion. It was different on a former occasion, when He was abused at the close of the ecclesiastical trial. Then it was His prophetic office that was turned into ridicule: "when they had blindfolded Him, they struck Him on the face and asked Him, saying, Prophesy who is it that smote thee." Here, on the other hand, the ridicule was directed against Him entirely on the ground of His claiming to be a king. The soldiers considered it an absurdity and a joke that one apparently so mean, friendless and powerless should make any such pretensions.

Many a time since then has the same derision been awakened by this claim of Christ. He is the King of nations. But earthly kings and statesmen have ridiculed the idea that His will and His law should control them in their schemes and ambitions. Even where His authority is nominally acknowledged, both aristocracies and democracies are slow to recognise that their legislation and customs should be regulated by His words. He is King of the Church. Andrew Melville told King James: "There are two kings and two kingdoms in Scotland; there is King James, the head of this commonwealth, and there is Christ Jesus, the King of the Church, whose subject James VI. is, and of whose kingdom he is not a king, nor a lord, nor a head, but a member." The entire history of the Scottish Church has been one long struggle to maintain this truth; but the struggle has frequently been carried on in the face of opposition almost as scornful as that which assailed Jesus in Pilate's palace. Most vital of all is the acknowledgment of Christ's kingship in the realm of the individual life; but it is here that His will is most resisted. In words we acknowledge allegiance to Him; but in which of us has the victory over the flesh been so complete that His full claim has been conceded, to have the arrangement of our business and our leisure and to dictate what is to be done with our time, our means and our services?

A third lesson is to recognise that in what Jesus bore on this occasion He was suffering for us.

Of all the features of the scene the one that has most impressed the imagination of Christendom is the crown of thorns. It was something unusual, and brought out the ingenuity and wantonness of cruelty. Besides, as the wound of a thorn has been felt by everyone, it brings the pain of the Sufferer nearer to us than any other incident. But it is chiefly by its symbolism that it has laid hold of the Christian mind. When Adam and Eve were driven from the garden into the bleak and toilsome world, their doom was that the ground should bring forth to them thorns and thistles. Thorns were the sign of the curse; that is, of their banishment from God's presence and of all the sad and painful consequences following therefrom. And does not the thorn, staring from the naked bough of winter in threatening ugliness, lurking beneath the leaves or flowers of summer to wound the approaching hand, tearing the clothes or the flesh of the traveller who tries to make his way through the thicket, burning in the flesh where it has sunk, fitly stand for that side of life which we associate with sin—the side of care, fret, pain, disappointment, disease and death? In a word, it symbolises the curse. But it was the mission of Christ to bear the curse; and, as He lifted it on His own head, He took it off the world. He bore our sins and carried our sorrows.

Why is it that, when we think of the crown of thorns now, it is not only with horror and pity, but with an exultation which cannot be repressed? Because, cruel as was the soldiers' jest, there was a divine fitness in their act; and wisdom was, even through their sin, fulfilling her own intention. There are some persons with faces so handsome that the meanest dress, which would excite laughter or disgust if worn by others, looks well on them, and the merest shreds of ornament, stuck on them anyhow, are more attractive than the most elaborate toilets of persons less favoured by nature. And so about Christ there was something which converted into ornaments even the things flung at Him as insults. When they called Him the Friend of publicans and sinners, though they did it in derision, they were giving Him a title for which a hundred generations have loved Him; and so, when they put on His head the crown of thorns, they were unconsciously bestowing the noblest wreath that man could weave Him. Down through the ages Jesus passes, still wearing the crown of thorns; and His followers and lovers desire for Him no other diadem.

Fourthly, this scene teaches the lesson of patience in suffering.

I remember a saint whom it was my privilege to visit in the beginning of my life as a minister. Though poor and uneducated, she was a person of very unusual natural powers; her ideas were singularly original, and she had a charming pleasantness of wit. Though not very old, she knew that she was doomed to die; and the disease from which she was suffering was one of the most painful incident to humanity. Often, I remember, she would tell me, that, when the torture was at the worst, she lay thinking of the sufferings of the Saviour, and said to herself that the shooting pains were not so bad as the spikes of the thorns.

Christ's sufferings are a rebuke to our softness and self-pleasing. It is not, indeed, wrong to enjoy the comforts and the pleasures of life. God sends these; and, if we receive them with gratitude, they may lift us nearer to Himself. But we are too terrified to be parted from them and too afraid of pain and poverty. Especially ought the sufferings of Christ to brace us up to endure whatever of pain or reproach we may have to encounter for His sake. Many would like to be Christians, but are kept back from decision by dread of the laughter of profane companions or by the prospect of some worldly loss. But we cannot look at the suffering Saviour without being ashamed of such cowardly fears. If the crown of thorns now becomes Christ so well as to be the pride and the song of men and angels, be assured that any twig from that crown which we may have to wear will one day turn out to be our most dazzling ornament.

[1] A ministerial friend told me that he once, in the hearing of Dr. Andrew Bonar, made reference to some things in the life of St. Paul which seemed to him to betray on the part of the apostle a sense of humour. He was not very sure how Dr. Bonar might take such a remark, and at the close he asked if he agreed with him. "Not only," was the reply, "do I agree with you, but I go further: I think there are distinct traces of humour in the sayings and the conduct of our Lord;" and he proceeded to quote examples. Everyone is aware how Dr. Bonar himself knew how to combine with the profoundest reverence and saintliness a strain of delightful mirth; and the absence of this is the great defect of his otherwise charming autobiography.

CHAPTER VIII.

THE SHIPWRECK OF PILATE

We have lingered long at the judgment-seat of Pilate. Far too long. Pilate has detained us. He knew perfectly well, the first glance he bestowed on the case, what it was his duty to do. But, instead of acting at once on his conviction, he put off. Of such delay good seldom comes. Pilate gave temptation time to assail him. He resisted it, indeed; he fought hard and long against it; but he ought never to have given it the chance. And he miserably succumbed in the end.

I.

When Pilate delivered Jesus over to be scourged, it looked as if he had surrendered Him to the cross; and so in all probability the Jews thought, because scourging was the usual preliminary to crucifixion. He, however, had not yet abandoned the hope of saving Jesus: he was still secretly adhering to the proposal he had made, to chastise Him and then let Him go. Perhaps, if he retired into the palace while the scourging was taking place, his wife may have urged him to make a further effort on behalf of that Just Man.

At all events he came out on the platform, round which the Jews were still standing, and informed them that the case was not finished; and, as Jesus, whose scourging was now over, came forward, he turned round and, pointing to Him, exclaimed with deep emotion, "Behold the Man."

It was an involuntary expression of commiseration,[1] an appeal to the Jews to recognize the unreasonableness of proceeding further: Jesus was so obviously not such an one as they had tried to make Him out to be; at all events He had suffered enough.

But the Christian mind has in all ages felt in these words a sense deeper than Pilate intended. As Caiaphas was uttering a greater truth than he knew when he said it was expedient that one should die for the whole people, so in uttering this exclamation the governor was an unconscious prophet. Preachers in every subsequent age have adopted his words and, pointing to Jesus, cried, "Behold the Man!" Painters have chosen this moment, when Jesus came forth, bleeding from the cruel stripes and wearing the purple robe and crown of thorns, as the one in which to portray the Man of Sorrows; and many a priceless canvas bears the title *Ecce Homo*.

From Pilate's lips there fell two words which the world will never forget—the question, "What is truth?" and this exclamation, "Behold the Man!" And the one may be taken as the answer to the other. When the question, "What is truth?" is put with deep earnestness, what does it mean but this?—Who will make God known to us? who will clear up the mystery of existence? who will reveal to man his own destiny? And to these questions is there any answer but this; "Behold the Man"? He has shown to the sons of men what they ought to be; His is the perfect life, after which every human life ought to be fashioned; He has opened the gates of immortality and revealed the secrets of the other world. And, what is far more important, He has not only shown us what our life here and hereafter ought to be, but how the ideal may be realised. He is not only the image of perfection but the Saviour from sin. Therefore ought the world to turn to Him and "behold the Man."

II.

Pilate hoped that the sight of the sufferings of Jesus would move the hard hearts of His persecutors, as it had moved his own. But the only response to his appeal was, "Crucify Him, crucify Him." It is to be noted, however, that these cruel words now came from "the chief priests and officers." Apparently the common people were moved: they might have yielded, if their superiors had allowed them. But nothing could move those hard hearts; indeed, the sight of blood only inflamed them the more; and they felt certain that by sheer persistence they could break down Pilate's opposition.

He was at his wits' end and replied to them angrily, "Take ye Him and crucify Him; for I find no fault in Him"; meaning probably, that he was willing to yield the Prisoner up to their will, if they would take the responsibility of executing Him; if, indeed, he had in his mind any clear meaning and was not merely uttering an exclamation of annoyance.

They perceived that the critical moment had arrived, and at last they let out the true reason for which they desired His death: "We have a law, and by our law He ought to die, because He made Himself the Son of God."

This was the ground on which they had condemned Him themselves, though up to this point they had kept it concealed. They had not mentioned it, because they thought that Pilate would jeer at it. It had on him, however, a very different effect. All the morning he had been feeling uneasy; and the more he saw of Jesus the more he disliked the part he was playing. But now at length the mention of His claim to be the Son of God caused his fears to take a definite and alarming shape. It revived in his mind the stories, with which his own pagan religion was rife, of gods or sons of the gods who had sometimes appeared on earth in disguise. It was dangerous to have to do with them; for any injury inflicted on them, even unconsciously, might be terribly avenged. He had discerned in Jesus something mysterious and inexplicable: what if He were the son of Jehovah, the native deity of Palestine, as Castor and Pollux were sons of Jupiter? and might not Jehovah, if He were injured, blast the man who wronged Him with a curse? Such was the terror that flashed through his mind; and, taking Jesus once more inside the palace, he asked Him, with a mixture of awe and curiosity, "Whence art Thou?"

Jesus gave him no answer, but again retired into the majestic silence which at three points already had marked His trial. In the whole conduct of the Saviour in His sufferings there is nothing more sublime than these pauses; but it is not easy at every point to gauge the state of mind to which they were due. Why was Jesus silent at this point? Some have said, because it was impossible to answer the question. He could not have said either Yes or No; for, if He had said that God was His Father, Pilate would have understood the statement in a grossly pagan sense; and yet, to avoid this, He could not say that He was not the Son of God. So it was best to say nothing.

The true explanation, however, is simpler. Jesus would say nothing about whether He was the Son of God or not, because He did not wish to be released on this ground. Not as a son of God, but as an innocent man, which Pilate had again and again acknowledged Him to be, was He entitled to be set free; and His silence called upon Pilate to act on this acknowledgment.

The judge was more than ever astonished; and he was irritated a little at being thus treated. "Speakest Thou not unto me?" he asked, flushing; "knowest Thou not that I have power to crucify Thee and have power to release Thee?" Poor man! it was to be seen before many minutes had passed how much power he had. And what was this power of which he boasted? He spoke as if he had arbitrary discretion to do whatever he pleased. No just judge would make such a claim: justice takes from him the power to follow his own inclination if it be unjust. It was of this Jesus reminded him when He now answered with quiet dignity, "Thou couldest have no power at all against Me, unless it were given thee from above." [2] He reminds him that the power he wields is delegated by Heaven, and therefore not to be used according to his own caprice, but according to the dictates of justice. Yet He added, "Therefore he that delivered Me unto thee hath the greater sin." He acknowledged that Pilate was in a position in which he was compelled to try the case: he had not taken it up at his own hand, as the Jewish authorities had done.

Thus Jesus recognised all the difficulties of His judge's position and was willing to make for him every allowance. This was He whom Pilate had, a few minutes before, given over to torture. Was there ever such sublime and unselfish clemency? Could there have been a more complete triumph over resentment and irritation? If the silence of Christ was sublime, no less sublime, when He did speak, were His words.

III.

Pilate felt the greatness and the magnanimity of his Prisoner, and came forth determined at all hazards to set Him free. The Jews saw it in his face. And at length they brought out their last weapon, which they had been keeping in reserve and Pilate had been fearing all the time: they threatened to complain against him to the emperor; for this was the meaning of what they now cried: "If thou let this man go, thou art not Caesar's friend: whosoever maketh himself a king speaketh against Caesar."

There was nothing which a Roman provincial governor so much dreaded as a complaint lodged against him at Rome. And in Pilate's case such an accusation, for more reasons than one, would have been specially perilous. The imperial throne was occupied at the time by one who was a most suspicious master. Tiberius seemed to delight in humiliating and disgracing his subordinates. Besides, at this very period he was peculiarly dangerous. A diseased body, the punishment of vices long indulged, had made his mind gloomy and savage; in fact, he was little better than a madman—morose, suspicious and malicious. Nor was any charge so likely to inflame him as the one which they proposed to lay against Pilate. It was well known at Rome that the hope of a Messiah was spread throughout the East; and any provincial governor supposed to be favouring or even conniving at the claims of such a pretender would certainly be recalled, probably exiled, and possibly executed. *Amicus Caesaris*, "Caesar's friend," was one of the most coveted titles of a man in Pilate's position; and to be accused of acting as no friend of Caesar's could act was the most serious of all dangers.

But there was something else which lent point to the threat of the Jewish authorities: Pilate well knew that his administration could not bear the light of an investigation such as would inevitably follow a complaint from his subjects. It is a curious thing that in a secular writer of that age we find an account of another occasion on which this same threat was held over Pilate; and the writer who mentions it adds: "He was afraid that if a Jewish embassy were sent to Rome, they might discuss the many maladministrations of his government, his extortions, his unjust decrees, his inhuman punishments." [3] Such had been the character of Pilate's past life; and now, when he was going to do a humane and righteous act, it stayed his hand. There is nothing which so frustrates good resolutions and paralyzes noble efforts as the dead weight of past sins. Those who are acquainted with secret and discreditable chapters of a man's history are able, wielding this knowledge over his head, to say, Thou shalt not do this good act which thou wishest to do, or, Thou shalt do this evil and shameful thing which we bid thee. There are companies in which men cannot utter the fine, high-sounding things they would say elsewhere, because there are present those who know how their lives have contradicted them. What is it that mocks the generous thought rising in our minds, that silences the noble word on our lips, that paralyzes the forming energy of our actions? Is it not the internal whisper, Remember how you have failed before? This is the curse of past sin: it will not let us do the good we would.

But, if a man has thus committed himself by an evil past, what is he to do? What ought Pilate to have done? There is only one course. It is to summon together the resources of his manhood, defy consequences, and do the right forthwith, come what may. One step taken in loyalty to conscience, one word of confession spoken, and in a moment the power of the tyranny is broken, and the spellbound man is free to issue forth from the inglorious prison of the past.

Alas, Pilate was not equal to any such effort. For the sake of righteousness, for the sake of this impressive and innocent but obscure and friendless Galilean, to face a complaint at Rome and run the risk of exile and poverty—the man of the world's philosophy could not rise to any such height. He belonged to the world, whose fashion and favour, pleasures and comforts were the breath of his nostrils; and, when he heard the menace of his subjects, he surrendered at discretion.

Thus Jewish passion and persistency triumphed. Pilate resisted, but he was forced to yield inch by inch. He wished to do right; he felt the spell of Jesus; and it irritated him to have to go against his conscience, but his subjects compelled him to obey their wicked will. Yet the true reason of his failure was in himself—in the shallowness and worldliness of his own character, which this occasion laid bare to the very foundations.[4]

IV.

There was little more to do. The mind of Pilate was very savage and his heart very sore. He had been beaten and humiliated; and he would gladly inflict some humiliation on his opponents, if he could find a way. He ascended the judgment-seat, "in a place that is called the Pavement, but in the Hebrew Gabbatha"—an act similar in significance, I suppose, with our judges' habit, before pronouncing a death sentence, of putting on the black cap. Pointing to Jesus, he exclaimed, "Behold your King!" It was as much as to say that he believed this really to be their Messiah—this poor, bleeding, mishandled Man. He was trying to cut them with a taunt. And he succeeded: smarting with pain they shouted, "Away with Him! away with Him! crucify Him!" "What," he proceeded, "shall I crucify your King?" And, borne away with fury, they responded, "We have no king but Caesar." What a word to come from the representatives of a nation to which pertained "the adoption and the glory and the covenants and the giving of the law and the service of God and the promises!" It was the renouncement of their birthright, the abandonment of their destiny. Pilate well knew what it had cost their proud hearts thus to forswear the hopes of their fathers and acknowledge the right of their conqueror; but to compel them to swallow this bitter draught was some compensation for the cup of humiliation they had compelled him to drink. And he took them at their word.

[1] Perhaps also of admiration. Pilate had never before seen so impressive a specimen of humanity; and the contrast between the sweetness and majesty of His appearance and the indignities which He had suffered drew from him this involuntary exclamation. One recalls Shakespeare's words about Brutus:

> "His life was gentle, and the elements
> So mixed in him, that nature might stand up
> And say to all the world, This was a Man!"

[2] We are much tempted on account of the "therefore" to explain "from above" as referring to the Jewish tribunal.

[3] Philo.

[4] It is a striking illustration of the irony of history that Pilate was overtaken by the very fate to escape which he abandoned Jesus. Soon after the Crucifixion his subjects lodged a complaint against him at Rome. He was recalled from his province and never returned. Ultimately, it is said, he terminated his existence with his own hand, "wearied out with miseries." Many legends in subsequent centuries clustered about his name. Several spots were supposed to be haunted by his restless and despairing spirit, notably a spring in Switzerland on the top of Mount Pilatus, which was thought to have derived its name from him; but this is more than doubtful.

CHAPTER IX.

JUDAS ISCARIOT

To the civil trial of our Lord there is a sad appendix, as we have already had one to the ecclesiastical trial. Christ's great confession in the palace of the high priest was accompanied by the great denial of Peter outside; and the proceedings in the court of Pontius Pilate were accompanied by the final act of the treachery of Judas. Only in the latter case we are not able with the same accuracy to fix the circumstances of time and place.

I.

Judas is one of the darkest riddles of human history. In the Vision of Hell the poet Dante, after traversing the circles of the universe of woe, in which each separate kind of wickedness receives its peculiar punishment, arrives at last, in the company of his guide, at the nethermost circle of all, in the very bottom of the pit, where the worst of all sinners and the basest of all sins are undergoing retribution. It is a lake not of fire but of ice, beneath whose transparent surface are visible, fixed in painful postures, the figures of those who have betrayed their benefactors; because this, in Dante's estimation, is the worst of sins. In the midst of them stands out, vast and hideous, "the emperor who sways the realm of woe"—Satan himself; for this was the crime which lost him Paradise. And the next most conspicuous figure is Judas Iscariot. He is in the mouth of Satan, being champed and torn by his teeth as in a ponderous engine.

Such was the mediaeval view of this man and his crime. But in modern times opinion has swung round to the opposite extreme. Ours is an age of toleration, and one of its favourite occupations is the rehabilitation of evil reputations. Men and women who have stood for centuries in the pillory of history are being taken down; their cases are retried; and they are set up on pedestals of admiration. Sometimes this is done with justice, but is other cases it has been carried to absurdity. Nobody, it would appear, has ever been very bad; the criminals and scoundrels have been men whose motives have been misunderstood. Among those on whose behalf the attempt has thus been made to reverse the verdict of history is Judas Iscariot. Eighteen centuries had agreed to regard him as the meanest of mankind, but in our century he has been transmuted into a kind of hero. The theory is of German origin; but it was presented to the English public by De Quincey, who adorned it with all the persuasiveness of his meretricious genius.

It is held that the motive of Judas was totally different from the one hitherto supposed: it was not filthy lucre. The smallness of the price for which he sold his Master—it was less than four pounds of our money, though the value of this sum was much greater then—proves that there must have been another motive. The traditional conception is inconsistent with Christ's choice of him to be a disciple; and it is irreconcilable with the tragic greatness of his repentance. His view of Christ's enterprise was no doubt of a material cast: he expected Christ to be a king, and hoped to hold a high place in His court: but these ideas were common to all the disciples, who to the very end were waiting to see their Master throw off the cloak of His humble condition and take to Himself His great power and reign; only they left the time and the means in their Master's hands, not venturing to criticise His proceedings. Judas was not so patient. He was a man of energy and practicality, and he allowed himself to believe that he had discerned a defect in the character of his Master. Jesus was too spiritual and unworldly for the enterprise on which he had embarked—too much occupied with healing, preaching and speculating. These would be well enough when once the kingdom was established; but He was losing His opportunities. His delay had turned against Him the authoritative classes. One vast force, indeed, was still on His side—the enthusiasm of the populace—but even of it He was not taking advantage. When, on Palm Sunday, He was borne into the capital by a crowd throbbing with Messianic expectation, He seemed to have in His hand what Judas supposed to be the object of His life; but He did nothing, and the crowd dispersed, disappointed and disheartened. What Jesus required was to be precipitated into a situation where He would be compelled to act. He lacked energy and decision; but, if He were delivered into the hands of the authorities, who were known to be seeking His life, He could hesitate no longer. When they laid hands on Him, He would of course liberate Himself from them, and His miraculous power would exhibit itself in forms so irresistible as to awaken universal enthusiasm. Thus would His kingdom be set up in magnificence; and the man whom the king would delight to honour would surely be the humble follower by whose shrewdness and audacity the crisis had been brought about.

II.

Even if this were the true history of Judas, his conduct would not, perhaps, be as innocent as it looks. In the course of His life our Lord had frequently to deal with persons who attempted, from what appeared to themselves to be good motives, to interfere with His plans—to precipitate Him into action before His time or to restrain Him when His time had come—and He always resented such interference with indignation. Even His own mother was not spared when she played this part. To do God's will exactly, neither more nor less, neither anticipating it nor lagging behind it, was the inner-most principle of the life of Jesus; and He treated any interference with it as a suggestion of the Evil One.

Still the theory will not hold water. The Scriptures know nothing of it, and it is inconsistent with the tone of moral repulsion in which they speak of Judas. Besides, they assign a totally different motive. They affirm that Judas was a thief and stole out of the bag from which Jesus gave to the poor and supplied His own wants—a sacrilege which most thieves would have scorned. It is in entire accordance with this that the word with which he approached the Sanhedrim was, "How much will ye give me?" That he was willing to accept so little proves how strong his passion was.

It is altogether impossible that a character of this kind can have been combined with the generous although mistaken enthusiasm which the theory attributes to him.[1] But, on the other hand, the passion of avarice may easily have been nourished by brooding with disappointment on Messianic visions; and the theory of De Quincey may supply important hints for unravelling the mystery of his career.

There can be no doubt that at one time the life of Judas seemed full of promise. Jesus, who was so strict about permitting any to follow Him, would not have chosen him into the apostolic circle unless he had exhibited enthusiasm for His person and His cause. He well knew, indeed, that in his motives there was a selfish alloy; but this was the case with all His followers; and fellowship with Himself was the fire in which the alloy was to be purged out.

In the other apostles this process actually took place: they were refined by fellowship with Him. Their worldliness, indeed, remained to the end of His earthly career, but it was growing less and less; and other ties, stronger than their hopes of earthly glory, were slowly but surely binding them indissolubly to His cause. In Judas, on the contrary, the reverse process took place: what was good in him grew less and less, and at last the sole bond which held him to Christ was what he could make out of the connection.

When the suspicion first dawned on him that the hope of a Messianic kingdom was not to be fulfilled, the inner man of Judas underwent a critical change. This happened a year before the end, on the occasion when Christ resisted the attempt of His followers to take Him by force and make Him a king, and when many of His disciples went back and walked no more with Him. At that time Jesus warned Judas against the evil spirit which he was allowing to take possession of his mind by the strong saying, "Have I not chosen you twelve? and one of you is a devil." But the disciple did not heed the warning. Perhaps it was at this stage that he commenced to steal from the bag which he carried. He felt that he must have some tangible reward for following Christ, and he justified his peculation by saying to himself that what he was taking was infinitely less than he had been led to expect. He regarded himself as an ill-used man.

Under the practice of this secret sin his character could not but rapidly deteriorate. Jesus dropped a word of warning now and then; but it had the reverse of the desired effect. Judas knew that Jesus knew; and he grew to hate Him. This was by far the worst aspect of the case. The other disciples were becoming more and more attached to their Master, because they felt increasingly how much they owed Him; but Judas did not feel that he owed Him anything: on the contrary, his feeling was that he had been betrayed. Why should he not betray in turn? There may even have been an element of scorn in selling Christ for so little.

More than one of the Evangelists seem to connect the treachery of Judas directly with the scene at Bethany in which Mary anointed Jesus with costly ointment. Apparently this beautiful act brought all the evil in his heart to such a head that an outbreak could no longer be deferred. His spite found vent in the angry contention that the money ought to have been given to the poor. It was a large sum, off which he could have taken an unusually large slice of booty. But probably there was more in the occasion to incense Judas. To him this feasting and anointing, at the moment when the crisis of Christ's fortunes had obviously come, appeared sheer folly; as a practical man he despised it. It was manifest that the game was up; a leader loitering and dreaming in this fashion at the crisis of his fate was doomed. It was time to get out of the ship, for it was clearly sinking; but he would do so in such a way as to gratify his resentment, his scorn and his love of money all at once.

Thus the master-passion of Judas was nourished from potent springs. But, indeed, avarice in itself is one of the most powerful of motives. In the teaching of the pulpit it may seldom be noticed, but both in Scripture and in history it occupies a prominent place. It is questionable if anything else makes so many ill deeds to be done. Avarice breaks all the commandments. Often has it put the weapon into the hand of the murderer; in most countries of the world it has in every age made the ordinary business of the market-place a warfare of falsehood; the bodies of men and the hearts of women have been sold for gold. Why is it that gigantic wrongs flourish from age to age, and practices utterly indefensible are continued with the overwhelming sanction of society? It is because there is money in them. Avarice is a passion of demonic strength; but it may help us to keep it out of our hearts to remember that it was the sin of Judas.

III.

The repentance of Judas is alleged as the sign of a superior spirit. Certainly it is an indication of the goodness which he once possessed, because it is only by the light of a spark of goodness that the darkness of sin can be perceived; and the more the conscience has been enlightened the severer is the reaction when it is outraged. Those who have in any degree shared the company of

Christ can never afterwards be as if they had not enjoyed this privilege; and religion, if it does not save, will be the cruellest element in the soul's perdition.

It is not certain at what point the reaction in the mind of Judas set in.[2] There were many incidents of the trial well calculated to awaken in him a revulsion of feeling. At length, however, the retributive powers of conscience were thoroughly aroused—those powers which in all literature have formed the theme of the deepest tragedy; which in the Bible are typified by Cain, escaping as a fugitive and a vagabond from the cry of his brother's blood; which in Greek literature are shadowed forth by the terrible figures of the Eumenides, with gorgon faces and blood-dropping eyes, following silently but remorselessly those upon whose track they have been set; and which in Shakespeare are represented in the soul-curdling scenes of Macbeth and Richard III. He was seized with an uncontrollable desire to undo what he had done. The money, on which his heart had been set, was now like a spectre to his excited fancy. Every coin seemed to be an eye through which eternal justice was gazing at his crime or to have a tongue crying out for vengeance. As the murderer is irresistibly drawn back to the spot where his victim lies, he returned to the place where his deed of treachery had been transacted and, confronting those by whom he had been employed, handed back the money with the passionate confession, "I have betrayed innocent blood." But he had come to miserable comforters. With cynical disdain they asked, "What is that to us? See thou to that." They had been cordial enough to him when he had come before, but now, after the instrument has served their turn, they fling it contemptuously aside. The miserable man had to turn away from the scorn of the partners of his guilt; but he could keep the money no longer—it was burning in his hands—and, before escaping from the precincts, he flung it down. This is said to have happened in that part of the temple which could be entered only by the priests;[3] and he must either have made a rush across the forbidden threshold or availed himself of an open door to fling it in. Not only did he desire to be rid of it, but a passionate impulse urged him to leave with the priests their own share of the guilt.

Then he rushed away from the temple. But where was he going? Oh that it had been in him to flee to Christ—that, breaking through all obstacles and rules, he had rushed to Him wherever He was to be found and cast himself at His feet! What if the soldiers had cut him down? Then he would have been the martyr of penitence, and that very day he would have been with Christ in Paradise. Judas repented of his sin; he confessed it; he cast from him the reward of iniquity; but his penitence lacked the element which is most essential of all—he did not turn to God. True repentance is not the mere horror and excitement of a terrified conscience: it is the call of God; it is letting go the evil because the good has prevailed; it includes faith as well as fear.

IV.

The manner of his end is also used as an argument in favour of the more honourable view of Judas. The act of suicide is one which has not infrequently been invested with a glamour of romance, and to go out of life the Roman way, as it is called, has been considered, even by Christians, an evidence of unusual strength of mind. The very reverse is, however, the true character of suicide: except in those melancholy cases where the reason is impaired, it must be pronounced the most contemptible act of which a human being is capable. It is an escape from the burdens and responsibilities of existence; but these burdens and responsibilities are left to be borne by others, and along with them is left an intolerable heritage of shame. From a religious point of view it appears in a still worse light. Not only does the suicide, as even heathen writers have argued, desert the post of duty where Providence has placed him, but he virtually denies the character and even the existence of God. He denies His character, for, if he believed in His mercy and love, he would flee to instead of from Him; and he denies His existence, for no one who believed that he was to meet God on the other side of the veil would dare in this disorderly way to rush into His presence.

The mode of Judas' suicide was characteristically base. Hanging does not appear to have been at all usual among the Jews. In the entire Old Testament there is said to occur only a single case; and, strange to say, it is that of the man who, in the principal act of his life also, was the prototype of Judas. Ahithophel, the counsellor and friend of David, betrayed his master, as Judas betrayed Christ; and he came to the same ignominious end.

It would seem, further, that the hanging of Judas was accompanied with circumstances of unusual horror. This we gather from the account in the beginning of Acts.[4] The terms employed are obscure; but they probably signify that the suicidal act was attended by a clumsy accident, in consequence of which the body, being suspended over a precipice and suddenly dropped by the snapping of the rope, was mangled in a shocking manner, which made a profound impression on all who heard of it.[5]

And this sense of his end being accursed was further accentuated in the minds of the early Christians by the circumstance that the money for which he had sold Christ was eventually used for the purchase of a graveyard for burying strangers in. The priests, though they picked up the coins from the floor over which Judas had strewn them, did not, scrupulous men, consider them good enough to be put in the sacred treasury; so they applied them to this purpose. The public wit, hearing of it, dubbed the place the Field of Blood; and thus the cemetery became a kind of monument to the traitor, of which he took possession as the first of the outcasts for whom it was designed.

The world has agreed to regard Judas as the chief of sinners; but, in so judging, it has exceeded its prerogative. Man is not competent to judge his brother. The master-passion of Judas was a base one; Dante may be right in considering treachery the worst of crimes; and the supreme excellence of Christ affixes an unparalleled stigma to the injury inflicted on Him. But the motives of action are too hidden, and the history of every deed is too complicated, to justify us in saying who is the worst of men. It is not at all likely that those whom human opinion would rank highest in merit or saintliness will be assigned the same positions in the rewards of the last day; and it is just as unlikely that human estimates are right when they venture to assign the degrees of final condemnation. Two things it is our duty to do in regard to Judas: first, not so to palliate his sin as to blunt the healthy, natural abhorrence of it; and, secondly, not to think of him as a sinner apart and alone, with a nature so different from our own that to us he can be no example. But for the rest, there is only one verdict which is at once righteous, dignified and safe; and it is contained in the declaration of St. Peter, that he "went to his own place."

[1] Hanna, in *The Last Day of Our Lord's Passion,* attempts to combine both motives, but without being able really to unite them; they remain as distinct as oil and water.

[2] If, as St. Matthew seems to indicate, Judas disappeared from the scene long before the end of the trial, this is strongly against the theory of De Quincey, according to which he must have stayed to the last moment, hoping to see Jesus assert Himself.

[3] *En to nao.*

[4] St. Matthew knows best the beginning, St. Luke the end of the story.

[5] De Quincey's interpretation of the words as a description of mental anguish must be felt by every reader of the brilliant essay to be forced and unnatural.

CHAPTER X.

VIA DOLOROSA

We have finished the first part of our theme—the Trial of Jesus—and turn now to the second and more solemn part of it—His Death. The trial had been little better than a mockery of justice: on the part of the ecclesiastical authority it was a foregone conclusion, and on the part of the civil authority it was the surrender of a life acknowledged to be innocent to the ends of selfishness and policy. But at last it was over, and nothing remained but to carry the unjust sentence into execution. So the tribunal of Pilate was closed for the day; the precincts of the palace were deserted by the multitude; and the procession of death was formed.

I.

Persons condemned to death in modern times are allowed a few weeks, or at least days, to prepare for eternity; but Jesus was crucified the same day on which He was condemned. There was a merciful law of Rome in existence at the time, ordaining that ten days should intervene between the passing of a capital sentence and its execution; but either this was not intended for use in the provinces or Jesus was judged to be outside the scope of its mercy, because He had made Himself a king. At all events He was hurried straight from the judgment-seat to the place of execution, without opportunity for preparation or farewells.

Of course the sentence was carried out by the soldiers of Pilate. St. John, indeed, speaks as if Pilate had simply surrendered Him into the hands of the Jews, and they had seen to the execution. But this only means that the moral responsibility was theirs. They did everything in their power to identify themselves with the deed. So intent were they on the death of Jesus, that they could not leave the work to the proper parties, but followed the executioners and superintended their operations. The actual work, however, was performed by the hands of Roman soldiers with a centurion at their head.

In this country executions are now carried out in private, inside the walls of the prison in which the criminal has been confined. Not many years ago, however, they took place in public; and not many generations ago the procession of death made a tour of the public streets, that the condemned man might come under the observation and maledictions of as many of the public as possible. This also was the manner of Christ's death. Both among the Jews and the Romans executions took place outside the gate of the city. The traditional scene of Christ's death, over which the Church of the Holy Sepulchre is built, is inside the present walls, but those who believe in its authenticity maintain that it was outside the wall of that date. This, however, is extremely doubtful; and, indeed, it is quite uncertain outside which gate of the city the execution took place. The name Calvary or Golgotha probably indicates that the spot was a skull-like knoll; but there is no reason to think that it was a hill of the size supposed by designating it Mount Calvary. Indeed, there is no hill near any gate corresponding to the image in the popular imagination. In modern Jerusalem there is a street pointed out as the veritable *Via Dolorosa* along which the procession passed; but this also is more than doubtful. Like ancient Rome, ancient Jerusalem is buried beneath the rubbish of centuries.[1] From the scene of the trial to the supposed site of the execution is nearly a mile. And it is quite possible that Jesus may have had to travel as far or farther, while an ever-increasing multitude of spectators gathered round the advancing procession.

One special indignity connected with the punishment of crucifixion was that the condemned man had to carry on his back through the streets the cross upon which he was about to suffer. In pictures the cross of Jesus is generally represented as a lofty structure, such as a number of men would have been needed to carry; but the reality was something totally different: it was not much above the height of a man,[2] and there was just enough of wood to support the body. But the weight was considerable, and to carry it on the back which had been torn with scourging must have been excessively painful.

Another source of intense pain was the crown of thorns, if, indeed, He still wore it. We are told that before the procession set out towards Golgotha the robes of mockery were taken off and His own garments put on; but it is not said that the crown of thorns was removed.

Most cruel of all, however, was the shame. There was a kind of savage irony in making the man carry the implement on which he was to suffer; and, in point of fact, throughout classical literature this mode of punishment is a constant theme of savage banter and derision.[3]

There is evidence that the imagination of Jesus had occupied itself specially beforehand with this portion of His sufferings. Long before the end He had predicted the kind of death He should die; but even before these predictions had commenced He had described the sacrifices which would have to be made by those who became His disciples as cross-bearing—as if this were the last extreme of suffering and indignity. Did He so call it simply because His knowledge of the world informed Him of this as one of the greatest indignities of human life? or was it the foreknowledge that He Himself was to be one day in this position which coloured His language? We can hardly doubt that the latter was the case. And now the hour on which His imagination had dwelt was come, and in weakness and helplessness He had to bear the cross in the sight of thousands who regarded Him with scorn. To a noble spirit there is no trial more severe than shame—to be the object of cruel mirth and insolent triumph. Jesus had the lofty and refined self-consciousness of one who never once had needed to cringe or stoop. He loved and honoured men too much not to wish to be loved and honoured by them; He had enjoyed days of unbounded popularity, but now His soul was filled with reproach to the uttermost; and He could have appropriated the words of the Psalm, "I am a worm and no man; a reproach of men and despised of the people."

The reproach of Christ is all turned into glory now; and it is very difficult to realise how abject the reality was. Nothing perhaps brings this out so well as the fact that two robbers were sent away to be executed with Him. This has been regarded as a special insult offered to the Jews by Pilate, who wished to show how contemptuously he could treat One whom he affected to believe their king. But more likely it is an indication of how little more Christ was to the Roman officials than any one of the prisoners whom they put through their hands day by day. Pilate, no doubt, had been interested and puzzled more than usual; but, after all, Jesus was only one of many; His execution could be made part of the same job with that of the other prisoners on hand. And so the three, bearing their crosses, issued from the gates of the palace together and took the Dolorous Way.

II.

Though He bore His own cross out of the palace of Pilate, He was not able to carry it far. Either He sank beneath it on the road or He was proceeding with such slow and faltering steps that the soldiers, impatient of the delay, recognised that the burden must be removed from His shoulders. The severity of the scourging was in itself sufficient to account for this breakdown; but, besides, we are to consider the sleepless night through which He had passed, with its anxiety and abuse; and before it there had been the agony of Gethsemane. No wonder His exhaustion had reached a point at which it was absolutely impossible for Him to proceed farther with such a burden.

One or two of the soldiers might have relieved Him; but, in the spirit of horseplay and mischief which had characterised their part of the proceedings from the moment when Christ fell into their hands, they lay hold of a casual passer-by and requisitioned his services for the purpose. He was coming in from the region beyond the gate as they were going out, and they acted under the sanction of military law or custom.

To the man it must have been an extreme annoyance and indignity. Doubtless he was bent on business of his own, which had to be deferred. His family or his friends might be waiting for him, but he was turned the opposite way. To touch the instrument of death was as revolting to him as it would be to us to handle the hangman's rope; perhaps more so, because it was Passover time, and this would make him ceremonially unclean. It was a jest of the soldiers, and he was their laughing-stock. As he walked by the side of the robbers, it looked as if he were on the way to execution himself.

This is a lively image of the cross-bearing to which the followers of Christ are called. We are wont to speak of trouble of any kind as a cross; and doubtless any kind of trouble may be borne bravely in the name of Christ. But, properly speaking, the cross of Christ is what is borne in the act of confessing Him or for the sake of His work. When anyone makes a stand for principle, because he is a Christian, and takes the consequences in the shape of scorn or loss, this is the cross of Christ. The pain you may feel in speaking to another in Christ's name, the sacrifice of comfort or time you may make in engaging in Christian work, the self-denial you exercise in giving of your means that the cause of Christ may spread at home or abroad, the reproach you may have to bear by identifying yourself with militant causes or with despised persons, because you believe they are on Christ's side—in such conduct lies the cross of Christ. It involves trouble, discomfort and sacrifice. One may fret under it, as Simon did; one may sink under it, as Jesus did Himself; it is ugly, painful, shameful often; but no disciple is without it. Our Master said, "He that taketh not his cross and followeth after Me is not worthy of Me."

III.

The one thing which makes Simon an imperfect type of the cross-bearer is that we are uncertain whether or not he bore the burden voluntarily. The Roman soldiers forced it on him; but was it force-work and nothing else?

Some have supposed that he was an adherent of Christ; but it is extremely improbable that, just at the moment when the soldiers needed someone for their purpose, one of the very few followers of Jesus should have appeared. The tone of the narrative seems rather to indicate that he was one who happened to be there by mere chance and had nothing to do with the proceedings till, against his will, he was made an actor in the drama.

He is said by the Evangelist to have been a Cyrenian, that is, an inhabitant of Cyrene, a city in North Africa. Strangers from this place are mentioned among those who were present soon after at the Feast of Pentecost, when the Holy Spirit descended on the Church in tongues of fire. And the probability is that Simon had, in a similar way, come from his distant home to the Passover.[4]

He had come on pilgrimage. Perhaps he was a devout soul, waiting for the consolation of Israel. In far Cyrene he may have been praying for the coming of the Messiah and, before setting out on this journey, pleading for a season of unusual blessing. God had heard and was going to answer his prayers, but in a way totally different from his expectations.

For apparently this *rencontre* issued in his salvation and in the salvation of his house. The Evangelist calls him familiarly "the father of Alexander and Rufus." Evidently the two sons were well known to those for whom St. Mark was writing; that is, they were members of the Christian circle. And there can be little doubt that the connection of his family with the Church was the result of this incident in the father's life. St. Mark wrote his Gospel for the Christians of Rome; and in the Epistle to the Romans one Rufus is mentioned as resident there along with his mother. This may be one of the sons of Simon. And in Acts xiii. 1 one Simeon—the same name as Simon—is mentioned along with a Lucius of Cyrene as a conspicuous Christian at Antioch: he is called Niger, or Black, a name not surprising for one who had been tanned by the hot sun of Africa. There are Alexanders mentioned elsewhere in the New Testament; but the name was common, and there is not much probability that any of them is to be identified with Simon's son. Still putting the details aside, we have sufficiently clear indications that in consequence of this incident Simon became a Christian.

Is it not a significant fact, proving that nothing happens by chance? Had Simon entered the city one hour sooner, or one hour later, his after history might have been entirely different. On the smallest circumstances the greatest results may hinge. A chance meeting may determine the weal or woe of a life. Doubtless to Simon this encounter seemed at the moment the most unfortunate incident that could have befallen him—an interruption, an annoyance and a humiliation; yet it turned out to be the gateway of life. Thus do blessings sometimes come in disguise, and out of an apparition, at the sight of which we cry out for fear, may suddenly issue the form of the Son of Man. But it was not Simon's own salvation only that was involved in this singular experience, but that of his family as well. How much may follow when Christ is revealed to any human soul! The salvation of those yet unborn may be involved in it—of children and children's children.

But think how blessed to Simon would appear in after days the cross-bearing which was at the time so bitter! No doubt it became the romance of his life. And to this day who can help envying him for being allowed to give his strength to the fainting Saviour and to remove the burden from that bleeding and smarting back? So for all men there is a day coming when any service they have done to Christ will be the memory of which they will be most proud. It will not be the recollection of the prizes we have won, the pleasures we have enjoyed, the discomforts we have escaped, that will come back to us with delight as we review life from its close; but, if we have denied ourselves and borne the cross for Christ's sake, the memory of that will be a pillow soft and satisfying for a dying head. In that day we shall wish that the minutes given to Christ's service had been years, and the pence pounds; and every cup of cold water and every word of sympathy and every act of self denial will be so pleasant to remember that we shall wish they had been multiplied a thousandfold.

[1] Interesting details in Ross's *Cradle of Christianity*.

[2] A soldier was able to reach up to the lips of Christ on the cross with a sponge on a reed.

[3] See Horace, S. ii. 7, 47; E. i. 16, 48.

[4] Many Jews, indeed, who had once been inhabitants of Cyrene lived in Jerusalem—old people, probably, who had come to lay their bones in holy ground; for we learn from an incidental notice in the Acts that they had a synagogue of their own in the city; and Simon may have been one of these. But the other is the more likely case.

CHAPTER XI.

THE DAUGHTERS OF JERUSALEM

There are many legends clustering round this portion of our Lord's history.

It is narrated, for example, that, when the divine Sufferer, burdened with the cross, was creeping along feebly and slowly, He leaned against the door of a house which stood in the way, when the occupier, striking a blow, commanded Him to hurry on; to which the Lord, turning to His assailant, replied, "Thou shall go on and never stop till I come again;" and to this day, unable to find either rest or death, the miserable man still posts over the earth, and shall continue doing so until the Lord's return. This is the legend of the Wandering Jew, which assumed many forms in the lore of other days and still plays a somewhat prominent part in literature. It is, I suppose, a fantastic representation, in the person of an individual, of the tragic fate of the Jewish race, which, since the day when it laid violent hands on the Son of God, has had no rest for the sole of its foot.

To another story of the *Via Dolorosa* as distinguished a place has been given in art as to the legend of the Wandering Jew in literature. Veronica, a lady in Jerusalem, seeing Christ, as He passed by, sinking beneath His burden, came out of her house and with a towel washed away the blood and perspiration from His face. And lo! when she examined the napkin with which the charitable act had been performed, it bore a perfect likeness of the Man of Sorrows. Some of the greatest painters have reproduced this scene, and it may be understood as teaching the lesson that even the commonest things in life, when employed in acts of mercy, are stamped with the image and superscription of Christ.

In Roman Catholic churches there may generally be seen round the walls a series of about a dozen pictures, taken from this part of our Lord's life. They are denominated the Stations of the Cross, because the worshippers, going round, stop to look and meditate on the different scenes. In Catholic countries the same idea is sometimes carried out on a more imposing scale. On a knoll or hill in the neighbourhood of a town three lofty crosses stand; the road to them through the town is called *Via Calvarii*, and at intervals along the way the scenes of our Lord's sad journey are represented by large frescoes or bas-reliefs.

But we really know for certain of only two incidents of the *Via Dolorosa*—that in which our Lord was relieved of His cross by Simon the Cyrenian and that, which we are now to consider, of the sympathetic daughters of Jerusalem.

I.

The reader of the history of our Lord in its last stages is sated with horrors. In some of the scenes through which we have recently accompanied Him we have seemed to be among demons rather than men. The mind longs for something to relieve the monstrous spectacles of fanatic hate and cold-blooded cruelty. Hence this scene is most welcome, in which a blink of sunshine falls on the path of woe, and we are assured that we need not lose faith in the human heart.

It was, indeed, a surprising demonstration. It would hardly have been credited, had it not there been made manifest, that Jesus had so strong a hold upon any section of the population of Jerusalem. In the capital He had always found the soil very unreceptive. Jerusalem was the headquarters of rabbinic learning and priestly arrogance—the home of the Pharisee and the Sadducee, who guided public opinion; and there, from first to last, He had made few adherents. It was in the provinces, especially in Galilee, that He had been the idol of the populace. It was by the Galilean pilgrims to the Passover that He was convoyed into the capital with shouts of Hosanna; but the inhabitants of the city stood coldly aloof, and before Pilate's judgment-seat they cried out, "Crucify Him, crucify Him!"

Yet now it turns out that He has touched the heart of one section at least even of this community: "There followed Him a great company of people and of women, which[1] also bewailed and lamented Him." Some have considered this so extraordinary that they have held these women to be Galileans; but Jesus addressed them as "daughters of Jerusalem." The Galilean men who had surrounded Him in His hour of triumph put in no appearance now in His hour of despair; but the women of Jerusalem broke away from the example of the men and paid the tribute of tears to His youth, character and sufferings. It is said that there was a Jewish law forbidding the showing of any sympathy to a condemned man; but, if so, this demonstration was all the more creditable to those who took part in it. The upwelling of their emotion was too sincere to be dammed back by barriers of law and custom.

It is said there is no instance in the Gospels of a woman being an enemy of Jesus. No woman deserted or betrayed, persecuted or opposed Him. But women followed Him, they ministered to Him of their substance, they washed His feet with tears, they anointed His head with spikenard; and now, when their husbands and brothers were hounding Him to death, they accompanied Him with weeping and wailing to the scene of martyrdom.[2]

It is a great testimony to the character of Christ on the one hand and to that of woman on the other. Woman's instinct told her, however dimly she at first apprehended the truth, that this was the Deliverer for her. Because, while

Christ is the Saviour of all, He has been specially the Saviour of woman. At His advent, her degradation being far deeper than that of men, she needed Him more; and, wherever His gospel has travelled since then, it has been the signal for her emancipation and redemption. His presence evokes all the tender and beautiful qualities which are latent in her nature; and under His influence her character experiences a transfiguration.[3]

It has, indeed, been contended that there was no great depth in the emotion of the daughters of Jerusalem; and we need not deny the fact. Their emotion was no outburst of faith and repentance, carrying with it revolutionary effects, as tears may sometimes be. It was an overflow of natural feeling, such as might have been caused by any pathetic instance of misfortune. It was not unlike the tears which may be still made to flow from the eyes of the tender-hearted by a moving account of the sufferings of Christ; and we know that such emotions are sometimes far from lasting. Our nature consists of several strata, of which emotion is the most superficial; and it is not enough that religion should operate in this uppermost region; it must be thrust down, through emotion, into the deeper regions, such as the conscience and the will, and catch hold and kindle there, before it can achieve the mastery of the entire being.

But this response of womanhood to Christ was a beginning; and therein lay its significance. It was to Him a foretaste of the splendid devotion which He was yet to receive from the womanhood of the world. It was as welcome to Him in that hour of desertion and reproach as is the sight of a tuft of grass to the thirsty traveller in the desert. The sounds of sympathy flowed over His soul as gratefully as the gift of Mary's love enveloped His senses when the house was filled with the odour of the ointment.

Thus in the *Via Dolorosa* Jesus experienced two alleviations of His suffering: the strength of a man relieved His body of the burden of the cross, and the pain of His soul was cooled by the sympathy of women. Is it not a parable— a parable of what men and women can do for Him still? Christ needs the strength of men—the strong arm, the vigorous hand, the shoulders that can bear the burden of His cause; He seeks from men the mind whose originality can plan what needs to be done, the resolute will that pushes the work on in spite of opposition, the liberal hand that gives ungrudgingly what is required for the progress and success of the Christian enterprise. From women he seeks sympathy and tears. They can give the sensibility which keeps the heart of the world from hardening; the secret knowledge which finds out the objects of Christian compassion and wins their confidence; the enthusiasm which burns like a fire at the heart of religious work. The influence of women is subtle and remote; but it is on this account all the more powerful; for they sit at the very fountains, where the river of human life is springing, and where a touch may determine its entire subsequent course.

II.

It has been allowed to condemned men in all ages to speak to the crowds assembled to witness their death. The dying speech used in this country to be a regular feature of executions. Even in ages of persecution the martyrs were usually allowed, as they ascended the ladder, to address the multitude; and these testimonies, some of which were of singular power and beauty, were treasured by the religious section of the community. It is nothing surprising, therefore, that Jesus should have addressed those who followed Him or should have been permitted to do so. No doubt He was at the last point of exhaustion, but, when He was relieved of the weight of the cross, He was able to rally strength sufficient for this effort. Pausing in the road and turning to the women, whose weeping and wailing were filling His ears, He addressed Himself to them.

His words are, in the first place, a revelation of Himself. They show what was demonstrated again and again during the crucifixion—how completely He could forget His own sufferings in care and anxiety for others. His sufferings had already been extreme; His soul had been filled with injustice and insult; at this very moment His body was quivering with pain and His mind darkened with the approach of still more atrocious agonies. Yet, when He heard behind Him the sobs of the daughters of Jerusalem, there rushed over His soul a wave of compassion in which for the moment His own troubles were submerged.

We see in His words, too, the depth and fervour of His patriotism. When He saw the tears of the women, the spectacle raised in His mind an image of the doom impending over the city whose daughters they were. Jerusalem, as has been already said, had always been extremely unresponsive to Him; she had played to Him an unmotherly part. None the less, however, did He feel for her the love of a loyal son. He had shown this a few days before, when, in the midst of His triumph, He paused on the brow of Olivet, where the city came into view, and burst into a flood of tears, accompanied with such a lyric cry of affection as has never been addressed to any other city on earth. Subsequently, sitting with His disciples over against the temple, He showed how well He foreknew the terrible fate which hung over the capital of His country, and how poignantly He felt it. The city's doom was nigh at hand: less than half a century distant: and it was to be unparalleled in its horror. The secular historian of it, himself a Jew, says in his narrative: "There has never been a race on earth, and there never will be one, whose sufferings can be matched with those of Jerusalem in the days of the siege." It was the foresight of this which made Jesus now say, "Daughters of Jerusalem, weep not for Me, but weep for yourselves and for your children."

His words, still further, reveal His consideration for women and children. The tears of the women displayed an appreciation and sympathy for Him such as the men were incapable of; but well did He deserve them, for His words show that He had a comprehension of women and a sympathy with them such as had never before existed in the world. With the force of the imagination and the heart He realised how, in the approaching siege, the heaviest end of the misery would fall on the female portion of the population, and how the mothers would be wounded through their children. In that country, where children were regarded as the crown and glory of womanhood, the currents of nature would be so completely reversed by the madness of hunger and pain that barrenness would be esteemed fortunate; and in a country where length of days had been considered the supreme blessing of life they would long and cry for sudden and early death.

So it actually turned out. An outstanding feature of the siege of Jerusalem, according to the secular historian, was the suffering of the women and children. Besides using every other device of warfare, the Romans deliberately resorted to starvation, and the inhabitants endured the uttermost extremities of hunger. So frenzied did the men become at last that every extra mouth requiring to be filled became an object of delirious suspicion, and the last morsels were snatched from the lips of the women and children. One is tempted to quote some of the stories of Josephus about this, but they are so awful that it would be scarcely decent to repeat them.

This was what the quick sympathy of Jesus enabled Him to divine; and His compassion gushed forth towards those who were to be the chief sufferers. Women and children—how irreverently they have been thought of, how callously and brutally treated, since history began! Yet they are always the majority of the human race. Praise be to Him who lifted them, and is still lifting them, out of the dust of degradation and ill-usage, and who put in on their behalf the plea of justice and mercy!

Finally, there was in the words addressed to the daughters of Jerusalem an exhortation to repentance. When Jesus said, "Weep for yourselves and for your children," He was referring not merely to the approaching calamities of the city, but to its guilt. This was indicated most clearly in the closing words of His address to them—"For if they do these things in a green tree, what shall be done in the dry?"

He could speak of Himself as a green tree. He was young and He was innocent; to this the tears of the women testified; there was no reason why He should die; yet God permitted all these things to happen to Him. The Jewish nation ought also to have been a green tree. God had planted and tended it; it had enjoyed every advantage; but, when He came seeking fruit on it, He found none. It was withered; the sap of virtue and godliness had gone out of it; it was dry and ready for the burning; and, when the enemy came to apply the firebrand, why should God interpose? Thus did Jesus attempt once more to awaken repentance. He wished to thrust the impressions of the daughters of Jerusalem down from the region of feeling into a deeper place. They had given Him tears of emotion; He desired, besides these, tears of contrition; for in religion nothing is accomplished till impression touches the conscience.

Whether any of them responded in earnest we cannot tell. Not many, it is to be feared. Nor can we tell whether by repentance the destruction of the Jewish state might still have been averted. At all events, the fire of invasion soon fell on the dry tree, and it was burnt up. And since then those who would not weep for their sins before the stroke of punishment fell have had to weep without ceasing. Visitors to Jerusalem at the present day are conducted to a spot called the Place of Wailing, where every Friday representatives of the race weep for the destruction of their city and temple.[4] This has gone on for centuries; and it is only a symbol of the cup of astonishment, filled to the brim, which has during many centuries been held to the lips of Israel. Sin must be wept for some time—if not before punishment has fallen, then after; if not in time, then in eternity. This is a lesson for all. And has not that final word of Jesus a meaning for us even more solemn than it had for those to whom it was first addressed—"If these things be done in a green tree, what shall be done in the dry?" If woe and anguish fell, as they did, even on the Son of God, when He was bearing the sins of the world, what will be the portion of those who have to bear their own?

[1] The participle refers to the women alone.

[2] "How slow we have been to ask our *sister* members to help us!—although we read of deaconesses in the early Church, and although we do not read of a single woman who was unkind and unfaithful to the Saviour while here upon earth. Men were diabolic in their cruelty to Him, but never did a woman betray Him, mock Him, desert Him, nor spit in His face. Many of them cheered Him on His way to the Cross, washing His feet with tears before men pierced them with nails, anointing His head with precious perfume in anticipation of the thorns with which men crowned Him. They wept with Him on the way to Calvary, and were true to Him to the very end. And are they not devoted and true to Him still? Why, then, have we been so long in calling for their services?"—E. HERBERT EVANS, D.D.

[3] Brace, *Gesta Christi*.

[4] Striking description in Baring-Gould, *The Passion of Jesus*, p. 75.

CHAPTER XII.

CALVARY

Anyone writing on the life of our Lord must many a time pause in secret and exclaim to himself, "It is high as heaven, what canst thou do? deeper than hell, what canst thou know?" But we have now arrived at the point where this sense of inadequacy falls most oppressively on the heart. To-day we are to see Christ crucified. But who is worthy to look at this sight? Who is able to speak of it? "Such knowledge is too wonderful for me; it is high; I cannot attain unto it." In the presence of such a subject one feels one's mind to be like some tiny creature at the bottom of the sea—as incapable of comprehending it all as is the crustacean of scooping up the Atlantic in its shell.

This spot to which we have come is the centre of all things. Here two eternities meet. The streams of ancient history converge here, and here the river of modern history takes its rise. The eyes of patriarchs and prophets strained forward to Calvary, and now the eyes of all generations and of all races look back to it. This is the end of all roads. The seeker after truth, who has explored the realms of knowledge, comes to Calvary and finds at last that he has reached the centre. The weary heart of man, that has wandered the world over in search of perfect sympathy and love, at last arrives here and finds rest. Think how many souls every Lord's Day, assembled in church and chapel and meeting-house, are thinking of Golgotha! how many eyes are turned thither every day from beds of sickness and chambers of death! "Lord, to whom can we go? Thou hast the words of eternal life."

Though, therefore, the theme is too high for us, yet we will venture forward. It is too high for human thought; yet nowhere else is the mind so exalted and ennobled. At Calvary poets have sung their sweetest strains, and artists seen their sublimest visions, and thinkers excogitated their noblest ideas. The crustacean lies at the bottom of the ocean, and the world of waters rolls above it; it cannot in its tiny shell comprehend these leagues upon leagues of solid translucent vastness; and yet the ocean fills its shell and causes its little body to throb with perfect happiness. And so, though we cannot take in all the meaning of the scene before which we stand, yet we can fill mind and heart with it to the brim, and, as it sends through our being the pulsations of a life divine, rejoice that it has a breadth and length, a height and depth, which pass understanding.

I.

The long journey through the streets to the place of execution was at length ended, and thereby the weary journeyings of the Sufferer came to a close.

The soldiers set about their preparations for the last act. But meanwhile a little incident occurred which the behaviour of Jesus filled with significance.

The wealthy ladies of Jerusalem had the practice of providing for those condemned to the awful punishment of crucifixion a soporific draught, composed of wine mixed with some narcotic like gall or myrrh,[1] to dull the senses and deaden the pain. It was a benevolent custom; and the cup was offered to all criminals, irrespective of their crimes. It was administered immediately before the frightful work of nailing the culprit to the tree commenced. This draught was handed to Jesus on His arrival at Golgotha. Exhausted with fatigue and burning with thirst, He grasped the cup eagerly and lifted it without suspicion to His lips. But, as soon as He tasted it and felt the fumes of the stupefying ingredient, He laid it down and would not drink.

It was a simple act, yet full of heroism. He was in that extremity of thirst when a person will drink almost anything; and He was face to face with outrageous torture. In subsequent times many of His own faithful martyrs, on their way to execution, gladly availed themselves of this merciful provision. But He would not allow His intellect to be clouded. His obedience was not yet complete; His plan was not fully wrought out; He would keep His taste for death pure. I have heard of a woman dying of a frightful malady, who, when she was pressed by those witnessing her agony to take an intoxicating draught, refused, saying, "No, I want to die sober." She had caught, I think, the spirit of Christ.

This is a very strange place in which to alight on the problem of the use and abuse of those products of nature or art which induce intoxication or stupefaction. Roots or juices with such properties have been known to nearly all races, the savage as well as the civilised; and they have played a great part in the life of mankind. Their history is one of the most curious. They are associated with the mysteries of false religions and with the phenomena of heathen prophecy and witchcraft; acting on the mind through the senses, they open up in it a region of mystery, horror and gloomy magnificence of which the normal man is unconscious. They have always been a favourite resource of the medical art, and in modern times, in such forms as opium and other better-known intoxicants, they have created some of the gravest moral problems.

On the wide question of the use of such substances as stimulants we need not at present enter; it is to their use for the opposite purpose of lowering consciousness that this incident draws attention. That in some cases this use is both merciful and permissible will not be denied. The discovery in our own day, by one of our own countrymen, of the use of chloroform is justly regarded as among the greatest benefits ever conferred on the human race. When the unconsciousness thus produced enables the surgeon to perform an operation which might not be possible at all without it, or when in the crisis of a fever the sleep induced by a narcotic gives the exhausted system power to continue the combat and saves the life, we can only be thankful that the science of to-day has such resources in its treasury.

On the other hand, however, there are grave offsets to these advantages. Millions of men and women resort to such substances in order to dull the nerves and cloud the brain during pain and sorrow which God intended them to face and bear with sober courage, as Jesus endured His on the cross. On the medical profession rests the responsibility of so using the power placed in their hands as not to destroy the dignity of the most solemn passages of life.[2] It will for ever remain true that pain and trial are the discipline of the soul; but to reel through these crises in the drowsy forgetfulness of intoxication is to miss the best chances of moral and spiritual development. Men and women are made perfect through suffering; but that suffering may do its work it must be felt. There is no greater misfortune than to bear too easily the strokes of God. A bereavement, for example, is sent to sanctify a home; but it may fail of its mission because the household is too busy, or because too many are coming and going, or because tongues, mistakenly kind and garrulous, chatter God's messenger out of doors. It is natural that physicians and kind friends should try to make sufferers forget their grief. But they may be too successful. Though the practice of the ladies of Jerusalem was a benevolent one, the gift mixed by their charitable hands appeared to our Lord a cup of temptation, and He resolutely put it aside.

II

All was now ready for the last act, and the soldiers started their ghastly work.

It is not my intention to harrow up the feelings of my readers with minute descriptions of the horrors of crucifixion.[3] Nothing would be easier, for it was an unspeakably awful form of death. Cicero, who was well acquainted with it, says: "It was the most cruel and shameful of all punishments." "Let it never," he adds, "come near the body of a Roman citizen; nay, not even near his thoughts or eyes or ears." It was the punishment reserved for slaves and for revolutionaries, whose end was intended to be marked by special infamy.

The cross was most probably of the form in which it is usually represented— an upright post crossed by a bar near the top. There were other two forms— that of the letter T and that of the letter X—but, as the accusation of Jesus is said to have been put up over His head, there must have been a projection above the bar on which His arms were outstretched. The arms were probably bound to the cross-beam, as without this the hands would have been torn through by the weight. And for a similar reason there was a piece of wood projecting from the middle of the upright beam, on which the body sat. The feet were either nailed separately or crossed the one over the other, with a nail through both. It is doubtful whether the body was affixed before or after the cross was elevated and planted in the ground. The head hung free, so that the dying man could both see and speak to those about the cross.

In modern executions the greatest pains are taken to make death as nearly as possible instantaneous, and any bungling which prolongs the agony excites indignation and horror in the public mind. But the most revolting feature of death by crucifixion was that the torture was deliberately prolonged. The victim usually lingered a whole day, sometimes two or three days, still retaining consciousness; while the burning of the wounds in the hands and feet, the uneasiness of the unnatural position, the oppression of overcharged veins and, above all, the intolerable thirst were constantly increasing. Jesus did not suffer so long; but He lingered for four or five hours.

I will not, however, proceed further in describing the sickening details. How far all these horrors may have been essential elements in His sufferings it would be difficult to say. Apart from the prophecies going before which had to be fulfilled, was it a matter of indifference what death He died? Would it have served equally well if He had been hanged or beheaded or stoned? We cannot tell. Only, when we know the secret of what His soul suffered, we can discern the fitness of the choice of the most shameful and painful of all forms of death for His body.[4]

The true sufferings of Christ were not physical, but internal. Looking on that Face, we see the shadow of a deeper woe than smarting wounds and raging thirst and a racking frame—the woe of slighted love, of a heart longing for fellowship but overwhelmed with hatred; the woe of insult and wrong, and of unspeakable sorrow for the fate of those who would not be saved. Nor is even this the deepest shadow. There was then in the heart of the Redeemer a woe to which no human words are adequate. He was dying for the sin of the world. He had taken on Himself the guilt of mankind, and was now engaged in the final struggle to put it away and annihilate it. On the cross was hanging not only the body of flesh and blood of the Man Christ Jesus, but at the same time His mystical body—that body of which He is the head and His people are the members. Through this body also the nails were driven, and on it death took its revenge. His people died with Him unto sin, that they might live for evermore.

This is the mystery, but it is also the glory of the scene. Till He hung on it, the cross was the symbol of slavery and vulgar wickedness; but He converted it into the symbol of heroism, self-sacrifice and salvation. It was only a wretched framework of coarse and blood-clotted beams, which it was a shame to touch; but since then the world has gloried in it; it has been carved in every form of beauty and every substance of price; it has been emblazoned on the flags of nations and engraved on the sceptres and diadems of kings.[5]

The cross was planted on Golgotha a dry, dead tree; but lo! it has blossomed like Aaron's rod; it has struck its roots deep down to the heart of the world, and sent its branches upwards, till to-day it fills the earth, and the nations rest beneath its shadow and eat of its pleasant fruits.[6]

III.

At length the ghastly preparations were completed; and in the greedy eyes of Jewish hatred the Saviour, whom they had hunted to death with the ferocity of bloodhounds, was exposed to full view. But the first triumphant glance of priests, Pharisees and populace met with a violent check; for above the Victim's head they saw something which cut them to the heart.

The practice of affixing to the apparatus of execution a description of the crime prevails in some countries to this day. In the Life of Gilmour of Mongolia there is a description of an execution which he witnessed in China; and in the cart which conveyed the condemned man to the scene of death a board was exhibited describing his misdeeds. The custom was a Roman one; and, besides, there was generally an official who walked in front of the procession of death and proclaimed the crimes of the condemned. No mention, however, of such a functionary appears in the Gospels; nor does the inscription appear to have been visible to all till it was affixed to the cross. It was fastened to the top of the upright beam; and Pilate made use of this opportunity to pay out the Jews for the annoyance they had caused him. He had parted from them in anger, for they had humiliated him; but he sent after them that which should be a drop of bitterness in their cup of triumph. When they were still at his judgment-seat, his last blow in his encounter with them had been to pretend to be convinced that Jesus really was their king. This insult he now prolonged by wording the inscription thus: "This is Jesus, the King of the Jews." It was as much as to say, This is what becomes of a Jewish king; this is what the Romans do with him; the king of this nation is a slave, a crucified criminal; and, if such be the king, what must the nation be whose king he is?

So enraged were the Jews that they sent a deputation to the governor to entreat him to alter the words. No doubt he was delighted to see them; for their coming proved how thoroughly his sarcasm had gone home. He only laughed at their petition and, assuming the grand air of authority which became no man so well as a Roman, dismissed them with the words, "What I have written I have written."

This looked like strength of will and character; but it was in reality only a covering for weakness. He had his will about the inscription—a trifle; but they had their will about the crucifixion. He was strong enough to browbeat them, but he was not strong enough to deny himself.

Yet, though the inscription of Pilate was in his own mind little more than a revengeful jest, there was in it a Divine purpose. "What I have written I have written," he said; but, had he known, he might almost have said, "What I have written God has written." Sometimes and at some places the atmosphere is so charged and electric with the Divine that inspiration alights and burns on everything; and never was this more true than at the cross. Pilate had already unconsciously been almost a prophet when, pointing to Jesus, he said, "Behold the Man"—a word which still preaches to the centuries. And now, after being a speaking prophet, he becomes, as has been quaintly remarked, a writing one too; for his pen was guided by a supernatural hand to indite the words, "This is Jesus, the King of the Jews."

It added greatly to the significance of the inscription that it was written in Hebrew and Greek and Latin. What Pilate intended thereby was to heighten the insult; he wished all the strangers present at the Passover to be able to read the inscription; for all of them who could read at all would know one of these three languages. But Providence intended something else. These are the three great languages of the ancient world—the representative languages. Hebrew is the tongue of religion, Greek that of culture, Latin the language of law and government; and Christ was declared King in them all. On His head are many crowns. He is King in the religious sphere—the King of salvation, holiness and love; He is King in the realm of culture—the treasures of art, of song, of literature, of philosophy belong to Him, and shall yet be all poured at His feet; He is King in the political sphere—King of kings and Lord of lords, entitled to rule in the social relationships, in trade and commerce, in all the activities of men. We see not yet, indeed, all things put under Him; but every day we see them more and more in the process of being put under Him. The name of Jesus is travelling everywhere over the earth; thousands are learning to pronounce it; millions are ready to die for it. And thus is the unconscious prophecy of Pilate still being fulfilled.

[1] One Evangelist says gall, another myrrh, and on this difference harmonists and their antagonists have spent their time; but surely it is not worth while.

[2] The distinction between the legitimate and the illegitimate use is not very easy to draw; but there is an obvious difference between destroying pain for an ulterior purpose and destroying it merely to save the feeling of the sufferer.

[3] On the details of crucifixion there is an extremely interesting and learned excursus in Zöckler's *Das Kreus Christi* (Beilage III.). Cicero's Verrine Orations contain a good deal that is valuable to a student of the Passion, especially in regard to scourging and crucifixion. Crucifixion was an extremely common form of punishment in the ancient world; but "the cross of the God-Man has put an end to the punishment of the crow."

[4] Zöckler maintains that crucifixion, while the most shameful, was not absolutely the most painful form of death.

[5] The appreciation of the significance of the Cross has gone on in two lines—the Artistic and the Doctrinal—both of which are followed out with varied learning in Zöckler's *Kreus Christi*.

The English reader may with great satisfaction trace the artistic development in Mrs. Jameson's *History of our Lord as exemplified in Works of Art*, where the following scheme is given of the varieties of treatment:—

"*Symbolical*, when the abstract personifications of the sun and moon, earth and ocean, are present.

"*Sacrificially symbolical*, when the Eucharistic cup is seen below the Cross, or the pelican feeding her young is placed above it.

"*Simply doctrinal*, when the Virgin and St. John stand on each side, as solemn witnesses; or our Lord is drinking the cup, sometimes literally so represented, given Him of the Father, while the lance opens the sacramental font.

"*Historically ideal*, as when the thieves are joined to the scene, and sorrowing angels throng the air.

"*Historically devotional*, as when the real features of the scene are preserved, and saints and devotees are introduced.

"*Legendary*, as when we see the Virgin fainting.

"*Allegorical and fantastic*, as when the tree is made the principal object, with its branches terminating in patriarchs and prophets, virtues and graces.

"*Realistic*, as when the mere event is rendered as through the eyes of an unenlightened looker-on.

"These and many other modes of conception account for the great diversity in the treatment of this subject; a further variety being given by the combination of two or more of these modes of treatment together; for instance, the pelican may be seen above the Cross giving her life's blood for her offspring; angels in attitudes of despair, bewailing the Second Person of the Trinity; or, in an ideal sacramental sense, catching the blood from His wounds—the Jews below looking on, as they really did, with contemptuous gestures and hardened hearts; the centurion acknowledging that this was really the Son of God, while the group of the fainting Virgin, supported by the Marys and St. John, adds legend to symbolism, ideality, and history."

In the study of the doctrinal development nothing is so important as the exegesis of the New Testament statements about the Cross; and this has been done in a masterly way by Dr. Dale in his work on the Atonement. What may be called the Philosophy of the Cross (to borrow a happy phrase of McCheyne Edgar's) came late. It is usually reckoned to have commenced with Anselm; and since the Reformation every great theologian has added his contribution. Yet the work is by no means completed. Indeed, at the present day there is no greater desideratum in theology than a philosophy of the Cross which would thoroughly satisfy the religious mind. Shallow theories abound; but the Church of Christ will never be able to rest in any theory which does not do justice, on the one hand, to the tremendously strong statements of Scripture on the subject and, on the other, to her own consciousness of unique and infinite obligation to the dying Saviour. Perhaps the most satisfactory expression of the Christian consciousness on the subject is to be found in the hymns of the Church, from the Te Deum down through Scotua Erigena and Fulbert of Chartres to Gerhardt and Toplady. See Schaff's *Christ in Song*.

A third line of development might be traced—the Practical—in martyrology, the history of missions, asceticism, and the like; and the spokesman of this branch of the truth is à Kempis, who, as Zöckler says, teaches his disciples to know poverty and humility as the roots of the tree of the Cross, labour and penitence as its bark, righteousness and mercy as its two principal branches, truth and doctrine as its precious leaves, chastity and obedience as its blossoms, temperance and discipline as its fragrance, and salvation and eternal life as its glorious fruit.

[6] When the Northern nations became Christian they transferred to the Cross the nobler ideas embodied in the mystic tree Igdrasil; and one of the commonest ideas of the mystical writers of the Middle Ages is the identification of the Cross as both the true tree of life and the true tree of knowledge.

CHAPTER XIII.

THE GROUPS ROUND THE CROSS

In the last chapter we saw the Son of Man nailed to the cursed tree. There He hung for hours, exposed, helpless, but conscious, looking out on the sea of faces assembled to behold His end. On the occasion of an execution a crowd gathers outside our jails merely to see the black flag run up which signals that the deed is done; and in the old days of public executions such an event always attracted an enormous crowd. No doubt it was the same in Jerusalem. When Jesus was put to death, it was Passover time, and the city was filled with multitudes of strangers, to whom any excitement was welcome. Besides, the case of Jesus had stirred both the capital and the entire country.[1]

The sight which the crowd had come to see was, we now know, the greatest ever witnessed in the universe. Angels and archangels were absorbed in it; millions of men and women are looking back to it to-day and every day. But what impressions did it make on those who saw it at the time? To ascertain this, let us look at three characteristic groups near the cross, whose feelings were shared in varying degrees by many around them.

I.

Look, first, at the group nearest the cross—that of the Roman soldiers.

In the Roman army it seems to have been a rule that, when executions were carried out by soldiers, the effects of the criminals fell as perquisites to those who did the work. Though many more soldiers were probably present on this occasion, the actual details of fixing the beam, handling the hammer and nails, hoisting the apparatus, and so forth, in the case of Jesus, fell to a quaternion of them. To these four, therefore, belonged all that was on Him; and they could at once proceed to divide the spoil, because in crucifixion the victim was stripped before being affixed to the cross—a trait of revolting shame.[2] A large, loose upper garment, a head-dress perhaps, a girdle and a pair of sandals, and, last of all, an under garment, such as Galilean peasants were wont to wear, which was all of a piece and had perhaps been knitted for Him by the loving fingers of His mother—these articles became the booty of the soldiers. They formed the entire property which Jesus had to leave, and the four soldiers were His heirs. Yet this was He who bequeathed the vastest legacy that ever has been left by any human being—a legacy ample enough to enrich the whole world. Only it was a spiritual legacy—of wisdom, of influence, of example.

The soldiers, their ghastly task over, sat down at the foot of the cross to divide their booty. They obtained from it not only profit but amusement; for, after dividing the articles as well as they could, they had to cast lots about the last, which they could not divide. One of them fetched some dice out of his pocket—gambling was a favourite pastime of Roman soldiers—and they settled the difficulty by a game. Look at them—chaffering, chattering, laughing; and, above their heads, not a yard away, that Figure. What a picture! The Son of God atoning for the sins of the world, whilst angels and glorified spirits crowd the walls of the celestial city to look down at the spectacle; and, within a yard of His sacred Person, the soldiers, in absolute apathy, gambling for these poor shreds of clothing! So much, and no more, did they perceive of the stupendous drama they were within touch of. For it is not only necessary to have a great sight to make an impression; quite as necessary is the seeing eye. There are those to whom this earth is sacred because Jesus Christ has trodden it; the sky is sacred because it has bent above Him; history is sacred because His name is inscribed on it; the daily tasks of life are all sacred because they can be done in His name. But are there not multitudes, even in Christian lands, who live as if Christ had never lived, and to whom the question has never occurred, What difference does it make to us that Jesus died in this world of which we are inhabitants?

II.

Look now at a second group, much more numerous than the first, consisting of the members of the Sanhedrim.

After condemning Jesus in their own court, they had accompanied Him through stage after stage of His civil trial, until at last they secured His condemnation at the tribunal of Pilate. When at last He was handed over to the executioners, it might have been expected that they would have been tired of the lengthy proceedings and glad to escape from the scene. But their passions had been thoroughly aroused, and their thirst for revenge was so deep that they could not allow the soldiers to do their own work, but, forgetful of dignity, accompanied the crowd to the place of execution and stayed to glut their eyes with the spectacle of their Victim's sufferings. Even after He was lifted up on the tree, they could not keep their tongues off Him or give Him the dying man's privilege of peace; but, losing all sense of propriety, they made insulting gestures and poured on Him insulting cries. Naturally the crowd followed their example, till not only the soldiers took it up, but even the thieves who were crucified with Him joined in. So that the crowd under His eyes became a sea of scorn, whose angry waves dashed up about His cross.

The line taken was to recall all the great names which He had claimed, or which had been applied to Him, and to contrast them with the position in which He now was. "The Son of God," "The Chosen of God," "The King of Israel," "The Christ," "The King of the Jews," "Thou that destroyest the temple and buildest it in three days"—with these epithets they pelted Him in every tone of mockery. They challenged Him to come down from the cross and they would believe Him. This was their most persistent cry—He had saved others, but Himself He could not save. They had always maintained that it was by the power of devils He wrought His miracles; but these evil powers are dangerous to palter with; they may lend their virtue for a time, but at last they appear to demand their price; at the most critical moment they leave him who has trusted them in the lurch. This was what had happened to Jesus; now at last the wizard's wand was broken and He could charm no more.

As they thus poured out the gall which had long been accumulating in their hearts, they did not notice that, in the multitude of their words, they were using the very terms attributed in the twenty-second Psalm to the enemies of the holy Sufferer: "He trusted in God; let Him deliver Him now, if He will have Him; for He said, I am the Son of God." Cold-blooded historians have doubted whether they could have made such a slip without noticing it; but, strange to say, there is an exact modern parallel. When one of the Swiss reformers was pleading before the papal court, the president interrupted him with the very words of Caiaphas to the Sanhedrim: "He hath spoken blasphemy: what further need have we of witnesses? What think ye?" and they all answered, "He is worthy of death"; without noticing, till he reminded them, that they were quoting Scripture.[3]

Jesus might have answered the cries of His enemies; because to one hanging on the cross it was possible not only to hear and see, but also to speak. However, He answered never a word—"when He was reviled, He reviled not again," "as a sheep before her shearers is dumb, so He opened not His mouth." This was not, however, because He did not feel. More painful than the nails which pierced His body were these missiles of malice shot at His mind. The human heart laid bare its basest and blackest depths under His very eyes; and all its foul scum was poured over Him.

Was it a temptation to Him, one wonders, when so often from every side the invitation was given Him to come down from the cross? This was substantially the same temptation as was addressed to Him at the opening of His career, when Satan urged Him to cast Himself from the pinnacle of the temple. It had haunted Him in various forms all His life through. And now it assails Him once more at the crisis of His fate. They thought His patience was impotence and His silence a confession of defeat. Why should He not let His glory blaze forth and confound them? How easily He could have done it! Yet no; He could not. They were quite right when they said, "He saved others, Himself He cannot save." Had He saved Himself, He would not have been the Saviour. Yet the power that kept Him on the cross was a far mightier one than would have been necessary to leave it. It was not by the nails through His hands and feet that He was held, nor by the ropes with which His arms were bound, nor by the soldiers watching Him; no, but by invisible bands—by the cords of redeeming love and by the constraint of a Divine design.

Of this, however, His enemies had no inkling. They were judging Him by the most heathenish standard. They had no idea of power but a material one, or of glory but a selfish one. The Saviour of their fancy was a political deliverer, not One who could save from sin. And to this day Christ hears the cry from more sides than one, "Come down from the cross, and we will believe Thee." It comes from the spiritually shallow, who have no sense of their own unworthiness or of the majesty and the rights of a holy God. They do not understand a theology of sin and punishment, of atonement and redemption; and all the deep significance of His death has to be taken out of Christianity before they will believe it. It comes, too, from the morally cowardly and the worldly-minded, who desire a religion without the cross. If Christianity were only a creed to believe, or a worship in whose celebration the aesthetic faculty might take delight, or a private path by which a man might pilgrim to heaven unnoticed, they would be delighted to believe it; but, because it means confessing Christ and bearing His reproach, mingling with His despised people and supporting His cause, they will have none of it. None can honour the cross of Christ who have not felt the humiliation of guilt and entered into the secret of humility.

III.

Let our attention now be directed to a third group. And again it is a comparatively small one.

As the eyes of Jesus wandered to and fro over the sea of faces upturned to His own—faces charged with every form and degree of hatred and contempt—was there no point on which they could linger with satisfaction? Yes, among the thorns there was one lily. On the outskirts of the crowd there stood a group of His acquaintances and of the women who followed Him from Galilee and ministered unto Him. Let us enumerate their honoured names, as far as they have been preserved—"Mary Magdalene, and Mary the mother of James and Joses [Transcriber's note: Joseph?], and the mother of Zebedee's children."

Their position, "afar off," probably indicates that they were in a state of fear. It was not safe to be too closely identified with One against whom the authorities cherished such implacable feelings; and they may have been quite right not to make themselves too conspicuous. Apart from the danger to which they might be exposed, they had a whole tempest of trouble in their hearts. As yet they knew not the Scriptures that He must rise again from the dead; and this collapse of the cause in which they had embarked their all for time and for eternity was a bewildering calamity. They had trusted that it had been He who should have redeemed Israel, and that He would live and reign over the redeemed race forever. And there He was, perishing before their eyes in defeat and shame. Their faith was at the very last ebb. Or say, rather, it survived only in the form of love. Bewildered as were their ideas, He had as firm a hold as ever on their hearts. They loved Him; they suffered with Him; they could have died for Him.

May we not believe that the eyes of Jesus, as long as they were able to see, turned often away from the brutal soldiers beneath His feet, and from the sea of distorted faces, to this distant group? In some respects, indeed, their aspect might be more trying to Him than even the hateful faces of His enemies; for sympathy will sometimes break down a strong heart that is proof against opposition. Yet this neighbourly sympathy and womanly love must, on the whole, have been a profound comfort and support. He was sustained all through His sufferings by the thought of the multitudes without number who would benefit from what He was enduring; but here before His eyes was an earnest of His reward; and in them He saw of the travail of His soul and was satisfied.

In these three groups, then, we see three predominant states of mind—in the soldiers apathy, in the Sanhedrim antipathy, in the Galileans sympathy.

Has it ever occurred to you to ask in which group you would have been had you been there? This is a searching question. Of course it is easy now to say which were right and which were wrong. It is always easy to admire the heroes and the causes of bygone days; but it is possible to do so and yet be apathetic or antipathetic to those of our own. Even the Roman soldiers at the foot of the cross admired Romulus and Cincinnatus and Brutus, though they had no feeling for One at their side greater than these. The Jews who were mocking Christ admired Moses and Samuel and Isaiah. Christ is still bearing His cross through the streets of the world, and is hanging exposed to contempt and ill-treatment; and it is possible to admire the Christ of the Bible and yet be persecuting and opposing the Christ of our own century. The Christ of to-day signifies the truth, the cause, the principles of Christ, and the men and women in whom these are embodied. We are either helping or hindering those movements on which Christ has set His heart; often, without being aware of it, men choose their sides and plan and speak and act either for or against Christ. This is the Passion of our own day, the Golgotha of our own city.

But it comes nearer than this. The living Christ Himself is still in the world: He comes to every door; His Spirit strives with every soul. And He still meets with these three kinds of treatment—apathy, antipathy, sympathy. As a magnet, passing over a heap of objects, causes those to move and spring out of the heap which are akin to itself, so redeeming love, as revealed in Christ, passing over the surface of mankind century after century, has the power so to move human hearts to the very depths that, kindling with admiration and desire, they spring up and attach themselves to Him. This response may be called faith, or love, or spirituality, or what you please; but it is the very test and touchstone of eternity, for it is separating men and women from the mass and making them one for ever with the life and the love of God.

[1] Keim strangely surmises that there was no great crowd; but this is impossible.

[2] As, however, the Jews would have objected to this, Edersheim argues—but not convincingly—that there must have been at least a slight covering.

[3] Süskind, *Passionsschule, in loc.*

CHAPTER XIV.

THE FIRST WORD FROM THE CROSS[1]

In the last chapter we saw the impressions made by the crucifixion on the different groups round the cross. On the soldiers, who did the deed, it made no impression at all; they were absolutely blind to the wonder and glory of the scene in which they were taking part. On the members of the Sanhedrim, and the others who thought with them, it had an extraordinary effect: the perfect revelation of goodness and spiritual beauty threw them into convulsions of angry opposition. Even the group of the friends of Jesus, standing afar off, saw only a very little way into the meaning of what was taking place before their eyes: the victory of their Master over sin, death and the world appeared to them a tragic defeat. So true is it, as I said, that, when something grand is to be seen, there is required not only the object but the seeing eye. The image in a mirror depends not only on the object reflected but on the quality and the configuration of the glass.

We wish, however, to see the scene enacted on Calvary in its true shape; and where shall we look? There was one mind there in which it was mirrored with perfect fidelity. If we could see the image of the crucifixion in the mind of Jesus Himself, this would reveal its true meaning.

But in what way can we ascertain how it appeared to Him, as from His painful station He looked forth upon the scene? The answer is to be found in the sentences which he uttered, as He hung, before His senses were stifled by the mists of death. These are like windows through which we can see what was passing in His mind. They are mere fragments, of course; yet they are charged with eternal significance. Words are always photographs, more or less true, of the mind which utters them; these were the truest words ever uttered, and He who uttered them stamped on them the image of Himself.

They are seven in number, and it will be to our advantage to linger on them; they are too precious to be taken summarily. The sayings of the dying are always impressive. We never forget the deathbed utterances of a parent or a bosom friend; the last words of famous men are treasured for ever. In Scripture Jacob, Joseph, Moses, and other patriarchal men are represented as having risen on their deathbeds far above themselves and spoken in the tones of a higher world; and in all nations a prophetic importance has been attached to the words of the dying. Now, these are the dying words of Christ; and, as all His words are like gold to silver in comparison with those of other men, so these, in comparison with the rest of His words, are as diamonds to gold.

In the First Word three things are noticeable—the Invocation, the Petition, and the Argument.

I.

It was not unusual for crucified persons to speak on the cross; but their words usually consisted of wild expressions of pain or bootless entreaties for release, curses against God or imprecations on those who had inflicted their sufferings. When Jesus had recovered from the swooning shock occasioned by the driving of the nails into His hands and feet, His first utterance was a prayer, and His first word "Father."

Was it not an unintentional condemnation of those who had affixed Him there? It was in the name of religion they had acted and in the name of God; but which of them was thus impregnated through and through with religion? which of them could pretend to a communion with God so close and habitual? Evidently it was because prayer was the natural language of Jesus that at this moment it leapt to His lips. It is a suspicious case when in any trial, especially an ecclesiastical one, the condemned is obviously a better man than the judges.

The word "Father," further, proved that the faith of Jesus was unshaken by all through which He had passed and by that which He was now enduring. When righteousness is trampled underfoot and wrong is triumphant, faith is tempted to ask if there is really a God, loving and wise, seated on the throne of the universe, or whether, on the contrary, all is the play of chance. When prosperity is turned suddenly into adversity and the structure of the plans and hopes of a life is tumbled in confusion to the ground, even the child of God is apt to kick against the Divine will. Great saints have been driven, by the pressure of pain and disappointment, to challenge God's righteousness in words which it is not lawful for a man to utter. But, when the fortunes of Jesus were at the blackest, when He was baited by a raging pack of wolf-like enemies, and when He was sinking into unplumbed abysses of pain and desertion, He still said "Father."

It was the apotheosis of faith, and to all time it will serve as an example; because it was gloriously vindicated. If ever the hand of the Creator seemed to be withdrawn from the rudder of the universe, and the course of human affairs to be driving down headlong into the gulf of confusion, it was when He who was the embodiment of moral beauty and worth had to die a shameful death as a malefactor. Could good by any possibility rise out of such an abyss of wrong? The salvation of the world came out of it; all that is noblest in history came out of it. This is the supreme lesson to God's children never to despair. All may be dark; everything may seem going to rack and ruin; evil may seem to be enthroned on the seat of God; yet God liveth; He sits above the tumult of the present; and He will bring forth the dawn from the womb of the darkness.

II.

The prayer which followed this invocation was still more remarkable: it was a prayer for the pardon of His enemies.

In the foregoing pages we have seen to what kind of treatment He was subjected from the arrest onwards—how the minions of authority struck and insulted Him, how the high priests twisted the forms of law to ensnare Him, how Herod disdained Him, how Pilate played fast and loose with His interests, how the mob howled at Him. Our hearts have burned with indignation as one depth of baseness has opened beneath another; and we have been unable to refrain from using hard language. The comment of Jesus on it all was, "Father, forgive them."

Long ago, indeed, He had taught men, "Love your enemies, bless them that curse you, do good to them that hate you, and pray for them which despitefully use you and persecute you." But this morality of the Sermon on the Mount had been considered, as the world still inclines to consider it, a beautiful dream. There have been many teachers who have said such beautiful things; but what a difference there is between preaching and practice! When you have been delighted with the sentiments of an author, it is frequently well that you know no more about him; because, if you chance to become acquainted with the facts of his own life, you experience a painful disillusionment. Have not students even of our own English literature in very recent times learned to be afraid to read the biographies of literary men, lest the beautiful structure of sentiments which they have gathered from their writings should be shattered by the truth about themselves? But Jesus practised what He taught. He is the one teacher of mankind in whom the sentiment and the act completely coincide. His doctrine was the very highest: too high it often seems for this world. But how much more practical it appears when we see it in action. He proved that it can be realised on earth when on the cross He prayed, "Father, forgive them."

Few of us, perhaps, know what it is to forgive. We have never been deeply wronged; very likely many of us have not a single enemy in the world. But those who have are aware how difficult it is; perhaps nothing else is more difficult. Revenge is one of the sweetest satisfactions to the natural heart. The law of the ancient world was, at least in practice, "Thou shalt love thy neighbour and hate thine enemy." Even saints, in the Old Testament, curse those who have persecuted and wronged them in terms of uncompromising severity. Had Jesus followed these and, as soon as He was able to speak, uttered to His Father a complaint in which the conduct of His enemies was branded in the terms it deserved, who would have ventured to find fault with Him? Even in that there might have been a revelation of God; because in the Divine nature there is a fire of wrath against sin. But how poor would such a revelation have been in comparison with the one which He now made. All His life He was revealing God; but now His time was short; and it was the very highest in God He had to make known.

In this word Christ revealed Himself; but at the same time He revealed the Father. All His life long the Father was in Him, but on the cross the divine life and character flamed in His human nature like the fire in the burning bush. It uttered itself in the word; "Father, forgive them"; and what did it tell? It told that God is love.

III.

The expiring Saviour backed up His prayer for the forgiveness of His enemies with the argument—"For they know not what they do."

This allows us to see further still into the divine depths of His love. The injured are generally alive only to their own side of the case; and they see only those circumstances which tend to place the conduct of the opposite party in the worst light. But at the moment when the pain inflicted by His enemies was at the worst Jesus was seeking excuses for their conduct.

The question has been raised how far the excuse which He made on their behalf applied. Could it be said of them all that they knew not what they were doing? Did not Judas know? did not the high priests know? did not Herod know? Apparently it was primarily to the soldiers who did the actual work of crucifixion that Jesus referred; because it was in the very midst of their work that the words were uttered, as may be seen in the narrative of St. Luke. The soldiers, the rude uninstructed instruments of the government, were the least guilty among the assailants of Jesus. Next to them, perhaps, came Pilate; and there were different stages and degrees down, through Herod and the Sanhedrim, to the unspeakable baseness of Judas. But St. Peter, in the beginning of Acts, expressly extends the plea of ignorance so far as to cover even the Sanhedrists—"And now, brethren, I wot that through ignorance ye did it, as did also your rulers"—and who will believe that the heart of the Saviour was less comprehensive than that of the disciple?

Let us not be putting limits to the divine mercy. It is true of every sinner, in some measure, that he knows not what he does. And to a true penitent, as he approaches the throne of mercy, it is a great consolation to be assured that this plea will be allowed. Penitent St. Paul was comforted with it: "God had mercy on me, because I did it ignorantly in unbelief." God knows all our weakness and blindness; men will not make allowance for it or even understand it; but He will understand it all, if we come to hide our guilty head in His bosom.

Of course this blessed truth may be perverted by an impenitent heart to its own undoing. There is no falser notion than that expressed in the French proverb, *Tout comprendre est tout pardonner* (To understand everything is to pardon everything), for it means that man is the mere creature of circumstances and has no real responsibility for his actions. How far our Lord was from this way of thinking is shown by the fact that He said, "Forgive them." He knew that they needed forgiveness; which implies that they were guilty. Indeed, it was His vivid apprehension of the danger to which their guilt exposed them that made Him forget His own sufferings and fling Himself between them and their fate.

It has been asked, Was this prayer answered? were the crucifiers of Jesus forgiven? To this it may be replied that a prayer for forgiveness cannot be answered without the co-operation of those prayed for. Unless they repent and seek pardon for themselves, how can God forgive them? The prayer of Jesus, therefore, meant that time should be granted them for repentance, and that they should be plied with providences and with preaching, to awaken their consciences. To punish so appalling a crime as the crucifixion of His Son, God might have caused the earth to open on the spot and swallow the sinners up. But no judgment of the kind took place. As Jesus had predicted, Jerusalem perished in indescribable throes of agony; but not till forty years after His death; and in this interval the pouring out of the Spirit at Pentecost took place, and the apostles began their preaching of the kingdom at Jerusalem, urgently calling the nation to repentance. Nor was their work in vain; for thousands believed. Even before the scene of the crucifixion terminated, one of the two thieves crucified along with Jesus, who had taken part in reviling Him, was converted; and the centurion who superintended the execution confessed Him as the Son of God. After all was over, multitudes who had beheld the sight went away smiting their breasts.[2] We have no reason to doubt, therefore, that even in this direct sense the prayer received an abundant answer.

But this was a prayer of a kind which may also be answered indirectly. Besides the effect which prayer has in procuring specific petitions, it acts reflexly on the spirit of the person who offers it, calming, sweetening, invigorating. Although some erroneously regard this as the only real answer that prayer can receive, denying that God can be moved by our petitions, yet we, who believe that more things are wrought by prayer, ought not to overlook this. By praying that His enemies might be forgiven, Jesus was enabled to drive back the spirits of anger and revenge which tried to force their way into His bosom, and preserved undisturbed the serenity of His soul. To ask God to forgive them was the triumphant ending of His own effort to forgive; and it is impossible to forgive without a delicious sense of deliverance and peace being shed abroad in the forgiving heart.

May we not add that part of the answer to this prayer has been its repetition age after age by the persecuted and wronged? St. Stephen led the way, in the article of death praying meekly after the fashion of his Master, "Lord, lay not this sin to their charge." Hundreds have followed. And day by day this prayer is diminishing the sum of bitterness and increasing the amount of love in the world.

[1] "Father, forgive them; for they know not what they do."

[2] Luke xxiii. 48.

CHAPTER XV.

THE SECOND WORD FROM THE CROSS[1]

I.

It is not said by whose arrangement it was that Jesus was hung between the two thieves. It may have been done by order of Pilate, who wished in this way to add point to the witticism which he had put into the inscription above the cross; or the arrangement may have been due to the Jewish officials, who followed their Victim to Golgotha and may have persuaded the soldiers to give Him this place, as an additional insult; or the soldiers may have done it of their own accord, simply because He was obviously the most notable of their prisoners.

The likelihood is that there was malice in it. Yet there was a divine purpose behind the wrath of man. Again and again one has to remark how, in these last scenes, every shred of action and every random word aimed at Jesus for the purpose of injuring and dishonouring Him so turned, instead, to honour, that in our eyes, now looking back, it shines on Him like a star. As a fire catches the lump of dirty coal or clot of filth that is flung into it, and converts it into a mass of light, so at this time there was that about Christ which transmuted the very insults hurled at Him into honours and charged even the incidents of His crucifixion which were most trivial in themselves with unspeakable meaning. The crown of thorns, the purple robe, Pilate's Ecce Homo, the inscription on the cross, the savage cries of the passers-by and other similar incidents, full at the time of malice, are now memories treasured by all who love the Saviour.

So His position between the thieves was ordained by God as well as by men. It was His right position. They had called Him long before "a friend of publicans and sinners;" and now, by crucifying Him between the thieves, they put the same idea into action. As, however, that nickname has become a title of everlasting honour, so has this insulting deed. Jesus came to the world to identify Himself with sinners; their cause was His, and He wrapped up His fate with theirs; He had lived among them, and it was meet that He should die among them. To this day He is in the midst of them; and the strange behaviour of the two between whom He hung that day was a prefigurement of what has been happening every day since: some sinners have believed on Him and been saved, while others have believed not: to the one His gospel is a savour of life unto life, to the other it is a savour of death unto death. So it is to be till the end; and on the great day when the whole history of this world shall be wound up He will still be in the midst; and the penitent will be on the one hand and the impenitent on the other.

But it was not in one way only that the divine wisdom overruled for high ends of its own the humiliating circumstance that Jesus was thus reckoned with the transgressors. It gave Him an opportunity of illustrating, at the very last moment, both the magnanimity of His own character and the nature of His mission; and at the moment when He needed it most it supplied Him with a cup of what had always been to Him the supreme joy of living—the bliss of doing good. As the parable of the Prodigal Son is an epitome of the whole teaching of Christ, so is the salvation of the thief on the cross the life of Christ in miniature.

II.

Both thieves appear to have joined in taunting Jesus, in imitation of the Sanhedrists. This has, indeed, been doubted or denied by those, of whom there have been many, who have experienced difficulty in understanding how so complete a revolution as the conversion of the penitent thief could take place in so short a time. Two of the Evangelists say that those crucified with Him reviled Him; but it is just possible grammatically to explain this as referring only to one of them; because sometimes an action is attributed to a class, though only one person of the class has done it.[2] The natural interpretation, however, is that both did it. It is likely enough, indeed, that the one who did not repent began it, and that the other joined in, less of his own accord than in imitation of his reckless associate. Very probably this was not the first time that he had been dragged into sin by the same attraction. His companion may have been his evil genius, who had ruined his life and brought him at last to this shameful end.

It was an awful extreme of wickedness to be engaged, so near their own end, in hurling opprobrious words at a fellow-sufferer. Of course, the very excess of pain made crucified persons reckless; and to be engaged doing anything, especially anything violent, helped to make them forget their agony. It mattered not who or what was the object of attack; they were reduced to the condition of tortured animals; and the trapped brute bites at anything which approaches it. This was the state of the impenitent thief. But the other drew back from his companion with horror. The very excess of sin overleaped itself; and for the first time he saw how vile a wretch he was. This was brought home to him by the contrast of the patience and peace of Jesus. His brutal companion had hitherto been his ideal; but now he perceives how base is his ferocious courage in comparison with the strength of Christ's serene endurance.

The desire to explain away the suddenness of the conversion has led to all sorts of conjectures as to the possibility of previous meetings between the thief and Christ. It is quite legitimate to dwell on what he had seen of the behaviour of Jesus from the moment when they were brought into contact in the crucifixion. He had heard Him pray for the forgiveness of His enemies; he had witnessed His demeanour on the way to Calvary and heard His words to the daughters of Jerusalem; the very cries of His enemies round the cross, when they cast in His teeth the titles which He had claimed or which had been attributed to Him, informed him what were the pretensions of Jesus; perhaps he may have witnessed and heard the trial before Pilate. But, when we attempt to go further back, we have nothing solid to found upon. Had he ever heard Jesus preach? Had he witnessed any of His miracles? How much did he know of the nature of His Kingdom, of which he spoke? Guesses may be made in answer to such questions, but they cannot be authenticated. I should be inclined with more confidence to look further back still. He may have come out of a pious home; he may have been a prodigal led astray by companions, and especially by the strong companion with whom he was now associated. As there was a weeping mother at the foot of the cross of Jesus, there may have been a heart-broken parent at the foot of that other cross also, whose prayers were yet going to be answered in a way surpassing her wildest hopes.

The question of the possibility of sudden conversion is generally argued with too much excitement on both sides to allow the facts to be recognised. Among us there may, in one sense, be said to be no such thing. Suppose anyone reading this page, who may know that he has not yet with his whole heart and soul turned to God, were to do so before turning the next leaf, would this be a sudden conversion? Why, the preparation for it has been going on for years. What has been the intention of all the religious instruction which you have received from your childhood, of the prayers offered on your behalf of the appeals which have moved you, of the strivings of God's Spirit, but to lead up to this result? Though your conversion were to take place this very hour, it would only be the last moment of a process which has gone on for years. Yet in a sense it would be sudden. And why should it not? What reason is there why your return to God should be further postponed? There are two experiences in religion which require to be carefully distinguished: there is the making of religious impressions on us by others from the outside—through instruction, example, appeal and the like; and there is the rise of religion within ourselves, when we turn round upon our impressions and make them our own. The former experience is long and slow, but the latter may be very sudden; and a very little thing may bring it about.

Another way in which it is possible to minimise the greatness of this conversion is by questioning the guilt of the man.[3] When he is called a thief, the name suggests a very common and degraded sinner; but it is pointed out that "robber" would be the correct name, and that probably he and his companion may have been revolutionaries, whose opposition to the Roman rule had driven them outside the pale of society, where, to win a subsistence, they had to resort to the trade of highwaymen; but in that country, tyrannised over by a despotic foreign power, those who attempted to raise the standard of revolt were sometimes far from ignoble characters, though the necessities of their position betrayed them into acts of violence. There is truth in this; and the penitent thief may not have been a sinner above all men. But his own words to his companion, "We receive the due reward of our deeds," point the other way. His memory was stained with acts for which he acknowledged that death was the lawful penalty. In short, there is no reason to doubt either that he was a great sinner or that he was suddenly changed. And therefore his example will always be an encouragement to the worst of sinners when they repent. It is common for penitents to be afraid to come to God, because their sins have been too great to be forgiven; but those who are encouraging them can point to cases like Manasseh, and Mary Magdalene, and the thief on the cross, and assure them that the mercy which sufficed for these is sufficient for all: "The blood of Jesus Christ, God's Son, cleanseth us from all sin."

The fear of those who endeavour to minimise the wonderfulness of this conversion is lest, if it be allowed that a man of the worst character could undergo so complete a change in so short a time on the very verge of the other world, men may be induced to put off their own salvation in the hope of availing themselves of a death-bed repentance. This is a just fear; and the grace of God has undoubtedly been sometimes thus abused. But it is an utter abuse. Those who allow themselves to be deceived with this reasoning believe that they can at any moment command penitence and faith, and that all the other feelings of religion will come to them whenever they choose to summon them. But does experience lead us to believe this? Are not the occasions, on the contrary, very rare when religion really moves irreligious men

> "We cannot kindle when we will
>   The fire that in the soul resides:
> The spirit breatheth and is still—
>   In mystery the soul abides."

Nor is it by any means a uniform experience that the approach of death awakens religious anxiety. The other thief is a solemn warning. Though face to face with death and in such close proximity to Jesus, he was only hardened and rendered more reckless than ever. And this is far more likely to be the fate of anyone who deliberately quenches the Spirit because he is trusting to a death-bed repentance.

Yet we will not allow the possible abuse of the truth to rob us of the glorious testimony contained in this incident to the grace of God. We set no limits to the invitation of the Saviour, "Him that cometh unto Me I will in no wise cast out." However late a sinner may be in coming, and however little time he may have in which to come, let him only come and he will not be cast out. There is no more critical test of theologies and theologians than the question what message they have to a dying person whose sins are unforgiven. If the salvation which a preacher has to offer is only a course of moral improvement, what can he have to say in such a place? We may be sure that our gospel is not the gospel of Him who comforted the penitent thief, unless we are able to offer even to a dying sinner a salvation immediate, joyful and complete.

How complete the revolution was in the penitent thief is shown by his own words. St. Paul in one place sums up Christianity in two things—repentance towards God and faith in the Lord Jesus Christ. And both of these we see in this penitent's words. His repentance towards God is brought out by what he said to his companion. "Dost thou not fear God?" he asked. He had himself forgotten God, no doubt, and put Him far away in the sinful past. But now God was near, and in the light of God he saw his own sinfulness. He confessed it, doing so not only in his secret mind but audibly. Thus he separated himself from it, as he did also from the companion who had led him astray, when he would not come with him on the path of penitence. Not less distinctly do His words to the Saviour manifest his faith in the Lord Jesus Christ. They are simple and humble: all he dared to expect was that, when Christ came into His kingdom, He would remember him. But they recognised the glory of Christ and expressed trust in Him. At the moment when the religious teachers of the nations thought that they had for ever destroyed Christ's claims, and even His own disciples had forsaken Him, this poor dying sinner believed in Him. "How clear," exclaims Calvin, "was the vision of the eyes which could thus see in death life, in ruin majesty, in shame glory, in defeat victory, in slavery royalty. I question if ever since the world began there has been so bright an example of faith." Luther is no less laudatory. "This," says he, "was for Christ a comfort like that supplied to Him by the angel in the garden. God could not allow His Son to be destitute of subjects, and now His Church survived in this one man. Where the faith of St. Peter broke off, the faith of the penitent thief commenced." And another[4] asks, "Did ever the new birth take place in so strange a cradle?"

III.

It is worth noting that it was not by words that Jesus converted this man. He did not address the penitent thief at all till the thief spoke to Him. The work of conviction was done before He uttered a word. Yet it was His work; and how did He do it? As St. Peter exhorted godly wives to convert their heathen husbands, when he wrote to them, "Likewise, ye wives, be in subjection to your own husbands, that, if any obey not the Word, they also may, without the Word, be won by the conversation (*i.e.*, behaviour) of the wives, while they behold your chaste conversation coupled with fear." It was by the impression of His patience, His innocence, His peace, and His magnanimity, that Jesus converted the man; and herein He has left us an example that we should follow in His steps.

But His words, when He did speak, added immensely to the impression. They were few, but every one of them expressed the Saviour.

The robber was thinking of some date far off when Christ might intervene in his behalf, but Christ says, "To-day." This was a prophecy that he would die that day, and not be allowed to linger for days, as crucified persons often were; and this was fulfilled. But it was, besides, a promise that as soon as death launched him out of time into eternity, Christ would be waiting there to receive him. "To-day thou shalt be with Me." All heaven is in these two last words. What do we really know of heaven, what do we wish to know, except that it is to be "with Christ"? Yet a little more was added—"in Paradise." Some have thought that in this phrase Christ was stooping to the conceptions of the penitent thief by using a popular expression for some happy place in the other world.[5] At least the word, which means a garden or park and was applied to the abode of our first parents in Eden, could not but call up in the consciousness of the dying man a scene of beauty, innocence and peace, where, washed clean from the defilement of his past errors, he would begin to exist again as a new creature. Even Christians have believed that the utmost that can be expected in the next world by a soul with a history like the robber's is, at least to begin with, to be consigned to the fires of purgatory. But far different is the grace of Christ: great and perfect is His work, and therefore ours is a full salvation.

This second word from the cross affords a rare glimpse into the divine glory of the Saviour; and it is all the more impressive that it is indirect. The thief, in the most solemn circumstances, spoke to Him as to a King and prayed to Him as to a God.[6] And how did He respond? Did He say, "Pray not to Me; I am a man like yourself, and I know as little of the unknown country into which we are both about to enter as you do"? This is what He ought to have answered, if He was no more than some make Him out to be. But He accepted the homage of His petitioner; He spoke of the world unseen as of a place native and familiar. He gave him to understand that He possessed as much influence there as he attributed to Him. This great sinner laid on Christ the weight of his soul, the weight of his sins, the weight of his eternity; and Christ accepted the burden.

[1] "To-day shalt thou be with Me in Paradise."

[2] So Augustin and many.

[3] Schleiermacher makes much of this; and, indeed, does everything in his power to minimise the moral miracle. The whole sermon is a specimen of his worst manner, when he rides away on some side issue and fails to expound the great central lessons of a subject.

[4] Tholuck.

[5] "In Biblical Hebrew the word is used for a choice garden but in the LXX. and the Apocalypse it is already used in our sense of Paradise."—EDERSHEIM.

[6] The word "Lord" in the robber's speech is, however, unauthentic.

CHAPTER XVI.

THE THIRD WORD FROM THE CROSS[1]

In the life of our Lord from first to last there is a strange blending of the majestic and the lowly. When a beam of His divine dignity is allowed to shine out and dazzle us, it is never long before there ensues some incident which reminds us that He is bone of our bone and flesh of our flesh; and, contrariwise, when He does anything which impressively brings home to us His humanity, there always follows something to remind us that He was greater than the sons of men. Thus at His birth He was laid in a manger; yet out on the pastures of Bethlehem angels sang His praise. Long afterwards He was asleep in the end of the boat, and so overcome with fatigue that He needed to be awakened to realise His danger; but immediately He rebuked the winds and the waves, and there was a great calm. When He saw the grief of Martha and Mary, "Jesus wept"; but only a few minutes afterwards He cried, "Lazarus, come forth," and He was obeyed. So it was to the very last. In studying the Second Word from the cross we saw Him opening the gates of Paradise to the penitent thief; to-day the Third Word will show Him to us as the Son of a woman, concerned in His dying hour for her bodily sustenance.

I.

The eye of Jesus, roving over the multitude whose component parts have been already described, lighted on His mother standing at the foot of the cross. In the words of the great mediaeval hymn, which is known to all by its opening words, *Stabat mater*, and from the fact that it has been set to music by such masters as Palestrina, Haydn and Rossini,

> "Beside the cross in tears
>   The woeful mother stood,
> Bent 'neath the weight of years,
>   And viewed His flowing blood;
> Her mind with grief was torn,
>   Her strength was ebbing fast,
> And through her heart forlorn
>   The sword of anguish passed."

When she carried her Infant into the temple in the pride of young motherhood, the venerable Simeon foretold that a sword would pierce through her own soul also. Often perhaps had she wondered, in happy days, what this mysterious prediction might mean. But now she knew, for the sword was smiting her, stab after stab.

It is always hard for a mother to see her son die. She naturally expects him to lay her head in the grave. Especially is this the case with the first-born, the son of her strength. Jesus was only thirty-three, and Mary must have reached the age when a mother most of all leans for support on a strong and loving son.

Far worse, however, was the death He was dying—the death of a criminal. Many mothers have had to suffer from the kind of death their children have died, when it has been in great agony or in otherwise distressing circumstances. But what mother's sufferings were ever equal to Mary's? There He hung before her eyes; but she was helpless. His wounds bled, but she dared not stanch them; His mouth was parched, but she could not moisten it. These outstretched arms used to clasp her neck; she used to fondle these pierced hands and feet. Ah! the nails pierced her as well as Him; the thorns round His brow were a circle of flame about her heart; the taunts flung at Him wounded her likewise.

But there was worse still—the sword cut deeper. Had not the angel told her before His birth, "He shall be great, and shall be called the Son of the Highest, and the Lord God shall give unto Him the throne of His father David; and He shall reign over the house of Jacob for ever; and of His kingdom there shall be no end"? This greatness, this throne, this crown, this kingdom—where were they? Once she had believed that she really was what the angel had called her—the most blessed of women—when she saw Him lying in her lap in His beautiful infancy, when the Shepherds and the Magi came to adore Him, and when Simeon and Anna recognised Him as the Messiah. After that ensued the long period of His obscurity in Nazareth. He was only the village carpenter; but she did not weary, for He was with her in their home; and she was confident that the greatness, the throne, the crown, the kingdom would all come in good time. At last His hour struck; and, casting down His tools and bidding her farewell, He went forth out of the little valley into the great world. It is all coming now, she said. Soon the news arrived of the words of grace and power He was speaking, of the multitudes following Him, of the nation being roused, and of the blind, the lame, the diseased, the bereaved who blessed Him for giving joy back to their lives, and blessed her who had borne Him. It is all coming to pass, she said. But then followed other news—of reaction, of opposition, of persecution. Her heart sank within her. She could not stay where she was. She left Nazareth and went away trembling to see what had happened. And now she stands at the foot of His cross. He is dying; and the greatness, the glory, and the kingdom have never come.

What could it mean? Had the angel been a deceiver, and God's word a lie, and all the wonders of His childhood a dream? We know the explanation now: Jesus was about to climb a far loftier throne than Mary had ever imagined, and the cross was the only road to it. Before many weeks were over Mary was to understand this too; but meantime it must have been dark as Egypt to her, and her heart must have been sorrowful even unto death. The sword had pierced very deep.

II.

There were other women with Mary beneath the cross—two of them Marys, like herself.[2] As an ancient father[3] has said, the weaker sex on this occasion proved itself the stronger. When the apostles had forsaken their Master and fled, these women were true to the last. Perhaps, indeed, their sex protected them. Women can venture into some places where men dare not go; and this is a talent which many women have used for rendering services to the Saviour which men could not have performed.

But there was one there who had not this protection, and who in venturing so near must have taken his life in his hand. St. John, I suppose, is included with the rest of the apostles in the sad statement that they all forsook their Master and fled. But, if so, his panic can only have lasted a moment. He was present at the very commencement of the trial; and here he still is with his Master at the last—the only one of all the Twelve. Perhaps, indeed, the acquaintance with the high-priest, which availed him to get into the palace where the trial took place, may still have operated in his favour. But it was most of all his greater devotion that brought him to his Master's side. He who had leaned on His breast could not stay away, whatever might be the danger. And he had his reward; for he was permitted to render a last service to Jesus amidst His agony, and he received from Him a token of confidence which by a heart like his must have been felt to be an unspeakable privilege and honour.

III.

It is most of all, however, with the impression made by the situation on Jesus Himself that we wish to acquaint ourselves.

He looked on His mother; and it was with an unpreoccupied eye, that was able to disengage its attention from every other object by which it was solicited. He was suffering at the time an extremity of pain which might have made Him insensible to everything beyond Himself. Or, if He had composure enough to think, a dying man has many things to reflect upon within his own mind. Christ, we know, had a whole world of interests to attend to; for now He was engaged in a final wrestle with the problem to which His whole life had been devoted. The prayer on behalf of His enemies does not surprise us so much, for it may be said to have been part of His office to intercede for sinners; nor His address to the penitent thief, for this also was quite in harmony with His work as the Saviour. But we do wonder that in such an hour He had leisure to attend to a domestic detail of ordinary life. Men who have been engaged in philanthropic and reformatory schemes have not infrequently been unmindful of the claims of their own families; and they have excused themselves, or excuse has been made for them, on the ground that the public interest predominated over the rights of their relatives. Now and then Jesus Himself spoke as if He took this view: He would not allow His plans to be interfered with even by His mother. But now He showed that, though He could not but refuse her unjust interference, He had never for a moment forgotten her just claims or her true interests. In spite of His greatness and in spite of His work, He still remained Mary's Son and bore to her an undying affection.

The words He spoke were, indeed, few; but they completely covered the case. Every word He uttered in that position was with great pain; therefore He could not say much. Besides, their very fewness imparted to them a kind of judicial dignity; as has been said, this was Christ's last will and testament. To His mother He said, "Woman, behold thy son," [4] indicating St. John with His eyes; and to the disciple He merely said, "Behold thy mother." It was simple, yet comprehensive; a plain, almost legal direction, and yet overflowing with love to both Mary and John.

It is supposed that Joseph, the husband of the Virgin, had died before our Lord's public career began, and that in Nazareth the weight of the household had fallen on the shoulders of Jesus. No doubt, during His years of preaching, He would tenderly care for His mother. But now He too was leaving her, and the widow would be without support. It was for this He had to provide.

He had no money to leave her; His earthly all, when He was crucified, consisted of the clothes He wore; and these fell to the soldiers. But it is one of the privileges of those who, though they may be poor themselves, make many rich with the gifts of truth, that they thereby win friends who are proud and eager to serve them or theirs. In committing His mother to St. John Jesus knew that the charge would be accepted not as a burden but a gift.

Why she did not go to the home of one of her other sons it is impossible to say. They were not yet believers, though soon afterwards they became so; but there may have been other reasons also, to us unknown.

At all events, it is easy to see how kind and considerate was the selection of St. John for this office. There are indications in the Gospels that St. John was wealthier, or at least more comfortable in his circumstances, than the rest of the Apostles; and this may have weighed with Jesus: He would not send His mother where she would feel herself to be a burden. It is highly probable also that St. John was unmarried. But there were deeper reasons. There was no arm on which His mother could lean so confidently as that of him who had leaned on her Son's breast. St. Peter, with his hot temper and rough fisherman's ways, would not have been nearly so eligible a choice. John and Mary were kindred spirits. They were especially one in their intense affection for Jesus. They would never tire of speaking to one another about Him. He honoured both of them in each other's eyes by giving them to one another in this way. If He gave Mary a great gift in giving her St. John for a son, He gave him no less a gift by giving him such a mother; for Mary could not but be an ornament to any home. Besides, did He not make St. John in a quite peculiar sense His own brother by substituting him in His own stead as the son of Mary?

The Evangelist says that from that hour John took her to his own home. Many have understood this to mean that he at once gently withdrew her from the spot, that she should not be agitated by seeing the death-throes of her Son, though he himself returned to Calvary. It is said by tradition that they lived together twelve years in Jerusalem, and that he refused to leave the city, even for the purpose of preaching the gospel, as long as Mary survived. Only after her death did he depart on those missionary travels which landed him in Ephesus and its neighbourhood, with which his later history is connected.

IV.

It is not difficult to read the lesson of this touching scene. From the pulpit of His cross Jesus preaches to all ages a sermon on the fifth commandment.

The heart of the mother of Jesus was pierced with a sword on account of His sufferings. It was a sharp weapon; but Mary had one thing on which to steady up her soul; it kept her calm even in the wildest moment of her grief—she knew He was innocent. He had always been pure, noble and good; she could be proud of Him even when they were crucifying Him. Many a mother's heart is pierced with anguish on account of a son's illness, or misfortunes, or early death; but she can bear it if she is not pierced with the poisoned sword. What is that? It is when she has to be ashamed of her child—when he is brought to ruin by his own misdeeds. This is a sorrow far worse than death.

How beautiful it is to see a mother wearing as her chief ornament the good name and the honourable success of a son! You who still have a mother or a father, let this be to you both a spur to exertion and a talisman against temptation. To some is accorded the rarer privilege of being able to support their parents in old age. And surely there is no sweeter memory in the world than the recollection of having been allowed to do this. "If any widow have children or nephews, let them learn first to show piety at home and to requite their parents; for that is good and acceptable before God. . . . But if any provide not for his own, and specially for those of his own house, he hath denied the faith, and is worse than an infidel." [5]

But this sermon, delivered from the pulpit of the cross, has a wider range. It informs us that our Saviour has a concern for our temporal as well as for our eternal interests. Even on the cross, where He was expiating the sin of the world, He was thinking of the comfort of His widowed mother. Let the needy and the deserted take courage from this, and cast all their care upon Him, for He careth for them. It is often an astonishment to see how widows especially are helped through. When they are left, with perhaps a number of little children, it seems incomprehensible how they can get on. Yet not infrequently their families turn out better than those where the father has been spared. One reason is, perhaps, that their children feel from the first that they must take a share of the responsibility, and this makes men and women of them. But the chief reason undoubtedly is that God fulfils His own promise to be a Father to the fatherless and a Husband to the widow, and that they have not been forgotten by Him who in the hour of His absorbing agony remembered Mary.

[1] "Woman, behold thy son . . . Behold thy mother."

[2] It is not certain whether John xix. 25 describes three women or four. Is the second Salome, John's mother?

[3] Chrysostom.

[4] "Woman" may mean sadly (proleptically), "Thou hast no son now."

[5] 1 Tim. v. 6, 8.

CHAPTER XVII.

THE FOURTH WORD FROM THE CROSS[1]

The Seven Words from the Cross may be divided into two groups. In the first three—namely, the prayer for His crucifiers, the word to the penitent thief, and the directions about His mother—our Lord was dealing with the interests of others; in the last four, to which we now pass, He was absorbed in His own concerns. This division is natural. Many a dying man, after arranging his affairs and saying his farewells, turns his face to the wall, to encounter death and be alone with God. It was highly characteristic of Jesus, however, before turning to His own things, first to mind the things of others.

Between these two groups of sayings there seems to have elapsed a long interval. From the sixth hour to the ninth Jesus was silent. And during this interval there was darkness over all the land. Of what precise nature this atmospheric effect may have been it is impossible at this distance to say. But the Evangelists, three of whom mention it, evidently consider it to have indicated in some sense the sympathy of nature with her Lord. It was as if the sun refused to look on such a deed of shame. It may be supposed that by this weird phenomenon the noises round the cross were in some degree hushed. At length the silence was broken by Christ Himself, who, in a loud voice, gave utterance to the Fourth Word from the cross. This was a word of astonishment and agony, yet also of victory.

I.

Of what nature had been the meditations of our Lord during the three hours of silence? Had He been in an ecstasy of communion with His heavenly Father? Not infrequently has this been vouchsafed to dying saints. And it has sometimes enabled them completely to overcome physical suffering. Martyrs have occasionally been so exalted at the last as to be able even to sing in the flames. It is with awe and astonishment we learn that the very opposite of this was the state of mind of Jesus. The word with which He burst out of the trance of silence may be taken as the index of what was going on in His mind during the preceding hours; and it is a cry out of the lowest depths of despair. Indeed, it is the most appalling sound that ever pierced the atmosphere of this earth. Familiar as it is to us, it cannot be heard by a sensitive ear even at this day without causing a cold shudder of terror. In the entire Bible there is no other sentence so difficult to explain. The first thought of a preacher, on coming to it, is to find some excuse for passing it by; and, after doing his utmost to expound it, he must still confess that it is quite beyond him. Yet there is a great reward in grappling with such difficult passages; for never does the truth impress us so profoundly as when we are made to feel that all the length which we are able to go is only into the shallows of the shore, while beyond our reach lies the great ocean.

Even in Christ's own mind the uppermost thought, when He uttered this cry, was one of astonishment. In Gethsemane, we are told, "He was sore amazed." And this is obviously the tone of this utterance also. We almost detect an accentuation of the "Thou" like that in the word with which the murdered Caesar fell. All His life Jesus had been accustomed to find Himself forsaken. The members of His own household early rejected Him. So did His fellow-townsmen in Nazareth. Ultimately the nation at large followed the same course. The multitudes that at one time followed Him wherever He went and hung upon His lips eventually took offence and went away. At last, in the crisis of His fate, one of His nearest followers betrayed Him and the rest forsook Him and fled. But in these disappointments, though He felt them keenly, He had always had one resource: He was always able, when rejected of men, to turn away from them and cast Himself with confidence on the breast of God. Disappointed of human love, He drank the more deeply of the love divine. He always knew that what He was doing or suffering was in accord with the will of God; His feelings kept constant time with the Divine heart; God's thoughts were His thoughts; He could clearly discern the divine intention leading through all the contradictions of His career to a sublime result. Therefore He could calmly say, even at the Last Supper, with reference to the impending desertion of the Twelve, "Behold, the hour cometh, yea, is now come, that ye shall be scattered, every man to his own, and shall leave Me alone; and yet I am not alone, because the Father is with Me." Now, however, the hour had come; and was this expectation fulfilled? They were scattered, as He had predicted, and He was left alone; but was He not alone? was the Father still with Him? His own words supply the answer: "My God, My God, why hast Thou forsaken Me?"

II.

Although the state of mind of our Lord on this occasion was so different from what we know to have been His habitual mood, yet it does not stand absolutely isolated in His history. We know of at least two experiences somewhat resembling it, and these may in some degree help us to its explanation. The first overtook Him on the occasion of the visit of certain Greeks at the beginning of the last week of His life. They had desired to see Him; but, when they were introduced by Andrew and Philip, Jesus, instead of being exhilarated, as might have been expected, was overcome with a spasm of pain, and groaned, "Now is My soul troubled, and what shall I say? Father, save Me from this hour." The sight of these visitors from the outside world made Him feel how grand and how congenial to Himself would have been a worldwide mission to the heathen, such as He might have undertaken had His life been prolonged; but this was impossible, because in the flower of His age He was to die. The other occasion was the Agony of Gethsemane. A careful and reverent study will reveal that this incident was the effort by which the will of Christ rose into unity with the will of His Father. It belongs to the very essence of human nature that it must grow from stage to stage; and the perfection of our Lord, just because it was human, had to realise itself on every step of a ladder of development. He was always both perfect on the stage which He had reached, and at the same time rising to a higher stage of perfection. Sometimes the step might be more easy, at other times more difficult; the step which He had to take in Gethsemane was supremely difficult; hence the effort and the pain which it cost. It seemed, however, in Gethsemane as if He had finally conquered, and it might have been expected that the mood of weakness and darkness could not come back. Yet it was to be permitted to return once more; and on the cross the attack was far more violent and prolonged than on either of the preceding occasions. Keeping in mind the light which these two previous accesses of the same mood may cast on this one, let us draw near reverently and see how far we may be able to penetrate into the mystery.

There can be little doubt that there was a physical element in it. He had now been a considerable time on the cross; and every minute the agony was increasing. The wounds in His hands and feet, exposed to the atmosphere and the sun, grew barked and hardened; the blood, impeded in its circulation, swelled in heart and brain, till these organs were like to burst; and the slightest attempt to move the body from the one intolerable posture caused pains to shoot along the quivering nerves. Bodily suffering clouds the brain and distorts the images formed on the mirror of the mind. Even the face of God, reflected there, may be turned to a shape of terror by the fumes of physical trouble.

The horror of mortal suffering may have been greater to Jesus than to other men, because of the fineness and sensitiveness of His physical organization. His body had never been coarsened with sin, and therefore death was utterly alien to it. The stream of physical life, which is one of the precious gifts of God, had poured through His frame in abundant and sunny tides. But now it was being withdrawn, and the counterflow had set in. The unity of a perfect nature was being violently torn asunder; and He felt Himself drifting away from the living world, which to Him had been so full of God's presence and goodness, into the pale, cold regions of inanity.[2] He did not belong to death; yet He was falling into death's grasp. No angel came to rescue Him; God interposed with no miracle to arrest the issue; He was abandoned to His fate.

There was more, however, it is easy to see, in the agony which prompted this cry than the merely physical. If in Gethsemane we have the effort of the will of Jesus, as it raised itself into unity with the will of the Father, we here see the effort of His mind as, amidst the confusion and contradictions of the cross, it finally rose into unity with the mind of God. This intellectual character of His pain is indicated by the word "Why." It is always painful when the creature has to say Why to the Creator. We believe that He is Sovereign of the world and Guide of our destiny, and that He urges forward the course of things in the reins of infinite wisdom and love. But, while this is the habitual and healthy sense of the human mind, especially when it is truly religious, there are crises, both in the great and in the little world, when faith fails. The world is out of joint; everything appears to have gone wrong; the reins seem to have slipped out of the hands of God and the chariot to be plunging forward uncontrolled; the course of things seems no more to be presided over by reason, but by a blind, if not a cruel fate. It is then that the poor human mind cries out Why. The entire book of Job is such a cry. Jeremiah cried Why to God in terms of startling boldness. In mortal pain, in bewildering disappointments, in bereavements which empty the heart and empty the world, millions have thus cried Why in every age. It seems an irreligious word. When Jeremiah says, "O Lord, Thou hast deceived me and I was deceived," or when Job demands, "Why did I not from the womb? why did I not give up the ghost when I came out of the belly?" it sounds like the voice of a blasphemer. But indeed it is into the most earnest and delicate souls that this despair is likeliest to slip. The ignorant, the frivolous and the time-serving are safe from it; for they are well enough satisfied with things as they are. Callous minds learn to be content without explanations. But the more deeply pious a mind is, the more jealous must it be for justice and the glory of God; the appearance of unwisdom in the government of the world shocks it; to be able to trace the footsteps of God's care is a necessity of its existence. Hence its pain when these evidences disappear. Now, all the contradictions and confusions of the world were focussed on Golgotha. Injustice was triumphant; innocence was scorned and crushed; everything was exactly the reverse of what it ought to have been. And all the millions of Whys which have risen from agonized souls, jealous for the honour of God but perplexed by His providence, were concentrated in the Why of Christ.

How near to us He is! Never perhaps in His whole life did He so completely identify Himself with His poor brethren of mankind. For here He comes down to stand by our side not only when we have to encounter pain and misfortune, bereavement and death, but when we are enduring that pain which is beyond all pains, that horror in whose presence the brain reels, and faith and love, the eyes of life, are put out—the horror of a universe without God, a universe which is one hideous, tumbling, crashing mass of confusion, with no reason to guide and no love to sustain it.

Can we advance a step farther into the mystery? The deepest question of all is whether the desertion of Jesus was subjective or objective—that is, whether He had only, on account of bodily weakness and a temporary obscuration of the inward vision, a sense of being abandoned, or whether, in any real sense, God had actually forsaken Him. Of course we are certain that God was infinitely well pleased with Him—never more so, surely, than when He was sacrificing Himself to the uttermost on behalf of others. But was there, at the same time, any outflashing against Him of the reverse side of the Divine nature—the lightning of the Divine wrath? Calvary was an awful revelation of the human heart, whose enmity was directed straight against the perfect revelation of the love of God in Christ. There the sin of man reached its climax and did its worst. What was done there against Christ, and against God in Him, was a kind of embodiment and quintessence of the sin of the whole world. And undoubtedly it was this which was pressing on Jesus; this was "the travail of His soul." He was looking close at sin's utmost hideousness; He was sickened with its contact; He was crushed with its brutality—crushed to death. Yet this human nature was His own; He was identified with it—bone of its bone, flesh of its flesh; and, as in a reprobate family an exquisitely delicate and refined sister may feel the whole weight of the debt and shame of the household to lie on herself, so He felt the unworthiness and hopelessness of the race as if they were His own; and, like the scapegoat on whose head the sins of the community were laid in the old dispensation, He went out into the land of forsakenness.

Thus far we may proceed, feeling that we have solid ground beneath our feet. But many have ventured farther. Even Luther and Calvin allowed themselves to say that in the hours which preceded this cry our Lord endured the torments of the damned. And Rambach, whose *Meditations on the Sufferings of Christ* have fed the piety of Germany for a hundred years, says: "God was now dealing with Him not as a loving and merciful father with his child, but as an offended and righteous judge with an evildoer. The heavenly Father now regards His Son as the greatest sinner to be found beneath the sun, and discharges on Him the whole weight of His wrath." But, if we were to make use of such language, we should be venturing beyond our depth. Much to be preferred is the modest comment of the holy and learned Bengel on our text: "In this fourth word from the cross our Saviour not only says that He has been delivered up into the hands of men, but that He has suffered at the hands of God something unutterable." Certainly there is here something unutterable. We have ventured into the mystery as far as we are able; but we know that we are yet only in the shallows near the shore; the unplumbed ocean lies beyond.

III.

It may appear an affectation to speak of this as in any sense a cry of victory. Yet, if what has just been said be true, this, which was the extreme moment of suffering, was also the supreme moment of achievement. As the flower, by being crushed, yields up its fragrant essence, so He, by taking into His heart the sin of the world, brought salvation to the world.

In point of fact, all history since has shown that it was in this very hour that Christ conquered the heart of mankind. Long before He had said, "I, if I be lifted up from the earth, will draw all men unto Me." And the correctness of this anticipation is matter of history. Christ on the cross has ever since then been the most fascinating object in the eyes of mankind. The mind and heart of humanity have been irresistibly attracted to Him, never weary of studying Him. And the utterance of this cry is the culminating moment to which the inquiring mind specially turns. Theology has its centre in the cross. Sometimes, indeed, it has been shy of it, and has divagated from it in wide circles; but, as soon as it becomes profound and humble again, it always returns.

Yes, when it becomes humble! Penitent souls are drawn to the cross, and the deeper their penitence the more are they at home. They stand beside the dying Saviour and say, This is what we ought to have suffered; our life was forfeited by our guilt; thus our blood deserved to flow; we might justly have been banished forever into the desert of forsakenness. But, as they thus make confession, their forfeited life is given back to them for Christ's sake, the peace of God is shed abroad in their hearts, and the new life of love and service begins. The supreme Christian rite brings us to this very spot and to this very moment: "This is My blood of the New Testament, shed for many for the remission of sins."

It was not, however, merely in this profound sense that this fourth word of the dying Saviour was a cry of victory. It was so, also, because it liberated Him from His depression. It has been said that when, at His encounter with the Greeks, He groaned, "Father, save Me from this hour," He immediately checked Himself with "Father, glorify Thy name"; likewise that in Gethsemane, when He prayed, "If it be possible, let this cup pass from Me," He hastened to add, "Nevertheless, not My will, but Thine be done"; but that on this occasion the cry of despair was followed by no word of resignation. This, however, is a mistake. The cry itself, though an utterance of despair, yet involved the strongest faith. See how He lays hold of the Eternal with both hands: "My God, My God!" It is a prayer: a thousand times He had turned to this resource In days of trial; and He does so in this supreme trouble. To do so cures despair. No one is forsaken who can pray, "My God." As one in deep water, feeling no bottom, makes a despairing plunge forward and lands on solid ground, so Jesus, in the very act of uttering His despair, overcame it. Feeling forsaken of God, He rushed into the arms of God; and these arms closed round Him in loving protection. Accordingly, as the darkness, which had brooded over all the land, disappeared at the ninth hour, so His mind emerged from eclipse; and, as we shall see, His last words were uttered in His usual mood of serenity.

[1] "My God, My God, why hast Thou forsaken Me?"

[2] Some of the Fathers thought of the separation of the divine from the human nature as taking place now.

CHAPTER XVIII.

THE FIFTH WORD FROM THE CROSS[1]

The fourth word from the cross we looked upon both as the climax of the struggle which had gone on in the mind of the divine Sufferer during the three hours of silence and darkness which preceded its utterance and as the liberation of His mind from that struggle. This view seems to be confirmed by the terms in which St. John introduces the Fifth Word—"After this, Jesus, knowing that all things were now accomplished,[2] that the Scripture might be fulfilled, saith, I thirst."

The phrase, "that the Scripture might be fulfilled," is usually connected with the words, "I thirst," as if the meaning were that He had said this fifth word in fulfilment of some prediction that He would do so; and the Old Testament is ransacked, without much result, for the prophetic words which may be supposed to be alluded to. It is better, however, to connect the phrase with what goes before—"Jesus, knowing that all things were now accomplished." It was only when His work, appointed by God and prescribed in Scripture, was completed, that He became sufficiently conscious of His bodily condition to say, "I thirst." Intense mental preoccupation has a tendency to cause the oblivion of bodily wants. Even the excitement of reading a fascinating book may keep at a distance for hours the sense of requiring sleep or food; and it is only when the reader comes out of the trance of absorption that he realises how spent he is. During the temptation in the wilderness Jesus was too absorbed to be aware of His bodily necessities; but, when the spiritual strain was removed, He "was afterward an hungered."

In the present instance, when He came out of His spiritual trance, it was thirst He became conscious of. I remember once talking with a German student who had served in the Franco-Prussian War. He was wounded in an engagement near Paris, and lay on the field unable to stir. He did not know exactly what was the nature of his wound, and he thought that he might be dying. The pain was intense; the wounded and dying were groaning round about him; the battle was still raging; and shots were falling and tearing up the ground in all directions. But after a time one agony, he told me, began to swallow up all the rest, and soon made him forget his wound, his danger and his neighbours. It was the agony of thirst. He would have given the world for a draught of water. This was the supreme distress of crucifixion. The agonies of the horrible punishment were of the most excruciating and complicated order; but, after a time, they all gathered into one central current, in which they were lost and swallowed up—that of devouring thirst; and it was this that drew from our Lord the fifth word.[3]

I.

This was the only cry of physical pain uttered by our Lord on the cross. As was remarked in a previous chapter, it was not uncommon for the victims of crucifixion, when the ghastly operation of nailing them to the tree began, to writhe and resist, and to indulge either in abject entreaties to be saved from the inevitable or in wild defiance of their fate. But at this stage Jesus uttered never a word of complaint. Afterwards also, in spite of the ever-increasing pain, He preserved absolute self-control. He was absorbed either in caring for others or in prayer to God.

It is a sublime example of patience. It rebukes our softness and intolerance of pain. How easily we are made to cry out; how peevish and ill-tempered we become under slight annoyances! A headache, a toothache, a cold, or some other slight affair, is supposed to be a sufficient justification for losing all self-control and making a whole household uncomfortable. Suffering does not always sanctify. It sours some tempers and makes them selfish and exacting. This is the besetting sin of invalids—to become absorbed in their own miseries and to make all about them the slaves of their caprices. But many triumph nobly over their temptation; and in this they are following the example of the suffering Saviour. There are sick-rooms which it is a privilege to visit. You may know that the place is a scene of excruciating pain; but on the pillow there lies a sweet, patient face; the voice is cheerful and thankful; and, instead of being self-absorbed, the mind is full of unselfish thoughts for others. I recall the description given by a friend of one such invalid's chamber, which used to be filled with the most beautiful cheerfulness and activity. At a certain time of year you might see in it quite an exhibition of stockings, pinafores, dresses and other pretty things, prepared for the children of a mission-school in India. By thinking of the needs of those children far away the invalid not only kept her own sufferings at bay, but created for herself delightful connections with God's work and God's people. Yet she was one who might easily have asserted the right to do nothing, and have taxed the patience and the services of those by whom she was surrounded.

But there is another lesson besides patience in this word of Christ. He only uttered one word of physical pain; but He did utter one. His self-control was not proud or sullen. There is a silence in suffering that is mere doggedness, when we screw our courage to the sticking-place and resolve that nobody shall hear any complaint from us. We succeed in being silent, but it is with a bad grace: there is no love or patience in our hearts, but only selfish determination. This is especially a temptation when anyone has injured us and we do not wish to let him see how much we have suffered, lest he should be gratified. Jesus was surrounded by those who had wantonly wronged Him; not only had they inflicted pain, but they had laughed and mocked at His sufferings. He might have resolved not on any account to show His feelings or at least to ask any kindness. It is sometimes more difficult to ask a favour than to grant one; it requires more of the spirit of forgiveness.[4] But not only did Jesus ask a favour: He expected to receive it. Shamefully as He had been treated by those to whom He had to appeal, He believed that there might still be some remains of goodness at the bottom of their hearts. All His life He had been wont to discover more good in the worst than others believed to exist, and to the last He remained true to His own faith. The maxim of the world is to take all men for rogues till the reverse has been proved. Especially when people have enemies, they believe the own very worst of them and paint their characters without a single streak of any colour but black. To those from whom we differ in opinion we attribute the basest motives and refuse to hear any good of them. But this is not the way of Christ: He believed there were some drops of the milk of human kindness even in the hard-hearted Roman soldiers; and He was not disappointed.[5]

II.

It is impossible to hear this pathetic cry, so expressive of helplessness and dependence, without recalling other words of our Lord to which it stands in marked contrast. Can this be He who, standing in Jerusalem not long before, surrounded with a great multitude, lifted up His voice and cried, "If any man thirst, let him come unto Me and drink"? Can it be He who, standing at the well of Jacob with the Samaritan woman and pointing to the springing fountain at their feet, said, "Whosoever drinketh of this water shall thirst again; but whosoever drinketh of the water that I shall give him shall never thirst; but the water that I shall give shall be in him a well of water springing up into everlasting life"? Can He who in words like these offered to quench the thirst of the world be the same who now whispers in mortal exhaustion, "I thirst"?

It is the same; and this is a contrast which runs through His whole life, the contrast between inward wealth and outward poverty. He was able to enrich the whole world, yet He had to be supported by the contributions of the women who followed Him; He could say, "I am the bread of life," yet He sometimes hungered for a meal; He could promise thrones and many mansions to those who believed on Him, yet He said Himself, "Foxes have holes, and the birds of the air have nests, yet the Son of man hath not where to lay His head."

In a materialistic age, when in so many circles money is the measure of the man, and when people are so excessively concerned about what they shall eat and what they shall drink and wherewithal they shall be clothed, it is worth while to bear this contrast in mind. Seldom have the noblest specimens of humanity been those who have been able to wallow in luxury; and the men who have enriched the world with the treasures of the mind have not infrequently been hardly able to procure daily bread. Our older boys may have seen on some of their school-books the name of Heyne. His is an immortal name in classical scholarship; but when he was a student, and even when he was enriching the literature of his country with splendid editions of the ancient writers, he was literally starving, and had sometimes to subsist on skins of apples and other offal picked up from the streets. Our own Samuel Johnson, to whose wisdom the whole globe is now a debtor, when engaged on some of his greatest works, had not shoes in which to go out, and did not know where his dinner was to come from. It would be easy from history to multiply instances of those who, though poor, yet have made many rich.

The inference is not, that one must be poor externally if one desires to be inwardly rich. The materially poor are not all spiritually rich by any means; multitudes of them, alas, are as poverty-stricken in mind and character as in physical condition. Perhaps one might even go so far as to say that as a rule the inwardly rich enjoy at least a competent portion of the good things of this life; for intelligence and character have even a market value, Money, too, can be made subservient to the highest aims of the soul. But what it is essential to remember is, that the inward is the true wealth, and that we must seek and obtain it, even, if necessary, at the sacrifice of the outward. If life is not to be impoverished and materialised, some in every age must make the choice between the inward and the outward wealth; and no one is worthy to be the servant of scholarship, art or religion who is not prepared for the choice should it fall to him. It is by the possession of intelligence, generosity and spiritual power that we enter into the higher ranks of manhood; and the most Christlike trait of all is to have the will and the ability to overflow in influences and activities which sweeten and elevate the lives of others.

III.

It would appear that some of those round the cross were opposed to granting the request of Jesus. Misunderstanding the fourth word,[6] they supposed He was calling for Elijah; and they proposed not to help Him even with a drink of water, in order to see whether or not Elijah would come to the rescue. But in one man the impulse of humanity was too strong, and he gave Jesus what He desired. We almost love the man for it, and we envy his office.

But the Saviour is still saying, "I thirst." How and where? Listen! "I was thirsty, and ye gave Me drink." "Lord, when saw we Thee athirst and gave Thee drink?" "Inasmuch as ye did it unto one of the least of these My brethren, ye did it unto Me." Wherever the brothers and sisters of Jesus are suffering, sitting in lonely rooms and wishing that somebody would come and visit them, or lying on beds of pain and needing somebody to come and ease the pillow or to reach the cup to the dry lips, there Christ is saying, "I thirst."

Perhaps He is saying it in vain. There are multitudes of professing Christians who never from end to end of the year visit any poor person. They never thread the obscure streets or ascend the grimy stairs in search of God's hidden ones. They have never acquired the art of cheering a dark home with a flower, or a hymn, or a diet, or the touch of a sympathetic hand and the smile of a healthy face. It would completely alter the Christianity of many if they could begin to do these lowly services; it would put reality into it, and it would bring into the heart a joy and exhilaration hitherto unknown. For Christ sees to it that none who thus serve Him lose their reward. An American friend told me that once, when travelling on the continent of Europe, he fell in with a fellow-countryman on board a Rhine steamer. They talked about America and soon confided to each other from which parts of the country they came, with other fragments of personal detail. They continued to travel for some days together, and my informant was so overwhelmed with kindness by his companion that at last he ventured to ask the reason. "Well," rejoined the other, "when the War was going on, I was serving in your native state; and one day our march lay through the town in which you have told me you were born. The march had been very prolonged; it was a day of intense heat; I was utterly fatigued and felt on the point of dying for thirst, when a kind woman came out of one of the houses and gave me a glass of cold water. And I have been trying to repay through you, her fellow-townsman, the kindness she showed to me." Does it not remind us of the great word of the Son of God, "Whosoever shall give to drink unto one of these little ones a cup of cold water only in the name of a disciple, verily I say unto you, he shall in no wise lose his reward"?

But is this not enough? Does anyone wish to get still nearer to Christ and hold the cup not only to Him in the person of His members but to His own very lips? Well, this is possible too. Jesus still says, "I thirst." He thirsts for love. He thirsts for prayer. He thirsts for service. He thirsts for holiness. Whenever the heart of a human being turns to Him with a genuine impulse of penitence, affection or consecration, the Saviour sees of the travail of His soul and is satisfied.

[1] "I thirst."

[2] *tetelestai*—the very word of Jesus Himself—"It is finished—" which may possibly have been fourth.

[3] He had by this time been on the cross for four hours or more. The arrest took place about midnight; the ecclesiastical trial terminated about sunrise; the proceedings before Pilate occupied perhaps from six to nine, or rather more; the crucifixion took place towards noon; from noon till three o'clock

darkness prevailed; and between this and sunset the death and burial took place. See Matt. xxvii. 1; Mark xv. 25, 33, 34, 42. St. John's statement of time, xix. 14, is a difficulty. He appears to reckon from a different starting-point. See Andrews' *Life of Our Lord* (new edition), pp. 545 ff. In the same passage St. John says, "It was the preparation of the passover"; does this mean the day before the feast commenced, or the day before the Sabbath of Passover Week? There are held to be other indications that St. John represents the crucifixion as having taken place the day before the Passover began, whereas the Synoptists place it the day after (especially John xviii. 28, where the question is whether "the passover" means the Paschal Lamb or the Chagigah, a portion of the feast belonging to the second day). On this question there is an extensive literature. See Andrews, 452-81, and Keim, vol. vi., pp. 195-219.

[4] "To be in too great a hurry to discharge an obligation is itself a kind of ingratitude."—LA ROCHEFOUCAULD.

[5] Hoffmann says that Jesus refused the intoxicating draught, before the crucifixion began, that His senses might be kept clear; and that now He accepted the refreshing draught for the same purpose.

[6] "Eli, Eli," etc.

CHAPTER XIX.

THE SIXTH WORD FROM THE CROSS[1]

Like the Fifth, the Sixth Word from the Cross is, in the Greek, literally a single word; and it has been often affirmed to be the greatest single word ever uttered. It may be said to comprehend in itself the salvation of the world; and thousands of human souls, in the agony of conviction or in the crisis of death, have laid hold of it as the drowning sailor grasps the life-buoy.

Sometimes it has been interpreted as merely the last sign of ebbing life: as if the meaning were, It is all over; this long agony of pain and weakness is done at last. But the dying words of Jesus were not spoken in this tone. The Fifth Word, we are expressly told, was uttered with a loud voice; so was the Seventh; and, although this is not expressly stated about the Sixth, the likelihood is that, in this respect, it resembled the other two. It was not a cry of defeat, but of victory.

Both the suffering of our Lord and His work were finishing together; and it is natural to suppose that He was referring to both. Suffering and work are the two sides of every life, the one predominating in some cases and the other in others. In the experience of Jesus both were prominent: He had both a great work to accomplish and He suffered greatly in the process of achieving it. But now both have been brought to a successful close; and this is what the Sixth Word expresses. It is, therefore, first, the Worker's Cry of Achievement; and, secondly, the Sufferer's Cry of Relief.

I.

Christ, when on earth, had a great work on hand, which was now finished.

This dying word carries us back to the first word from His lips which has been preserved to us: "Wist ye not that I must be about my Father's business?" Even at twelve years of age He already knew that there was a business entrusted to Him by His Father in heaven, about which His thoughts had to be occupied. We cannot perhaps say that then already He comprehended it in its whole extent. It was to grow upon Him with the development of His manhood. In lonely meditations in the fields and pastures of Nazareth it seized and inspired His mind. As He cultivated the life of prayer, it became more and more His settled purpose. The more He became acquainted with human nature, and with the character and the needs of His own age, the more clearly did it rise before Him. As He heard and read the Scriptures of the Old Testament, He saw it hinted and foreshadowed in type and symbol, in rite and institution, in law and prophets. There He found the programme of His life sketched out beforehand; and perhaps one of His uppermost thoughts, when He said, "It is finished," was that all which had been foretold about Him in the ancient Scriptures had been fulfilled.

After His public life commenced, the sense of being charged with a task which He had to fulfil was one of the master-thoughts of His life. It was written on His very face and bodily gait. He never had the easy, indeterminate air of one who does not know what He means to do in the world. "I have a baptism," He would say, "to be baptized with, and how am I straitened till it be accomplished." In a rapt moment, at the well of Sychar, after His interview with the Samaritan woman, when His disciples proffered Him food, He put it away from Him, saying, "I have meat to eat that ye know not of," and He added, "My meat is to do the will of Him that sent Me and to finish His work." On His last journey to Jerusalem, as He went on in front of His disciples, they were amazed and, as they followed, they were afraid. His purpose possessed Him; He was wholly in it, body, soul and spirit. He bestowed on it every scrap of power He possessed, and every moment of His time. Looking back now from the close of life, He has not to regret that any talent has been either abused or left unused. All have been husbanded for the one purpose and all lavished on the work.

What was this work of Christ? In what terms shall we express it? At all events it was a greater work than any other son of man has ever attempted. Men have attempted much, and some of them have given themselves to their chosen enterprises with extraordinary devotion and tenacity. The conqueror has devoted himself to his scheme of subduing the world; the patriot to the liberation of his country; the philosopher to the enlargement of the realm of knowledge; the inventor has rummaged with tireless industry among the secrets of nature; and the discoverer has risked his life in opening up untrodden continents and died with his face to his task. But none ever undertook a task worthy to be compared with that which engrossed the mind of Jesus.

It was a work for God with men, and it was a work for men with God.

The thought that it was a work for God, with which God had charged Him, was often in Christ's mouth, and this consciousness was one of the chief sources of His inspiration. "I must work the work of Him that sent Me while it is day," He would say; or, "Therefore doth my Father love Me, because I do always those things which please Him." And, at the close of His life-work, He said, in words closely related to those of our text, "I have glorified Thee on the earth, I have finished the work which Thou gavest Me to do." This was His task, to glorify God on the earth—to make known the Father to the children of men.

But just as obviously was it a work for men with God. This was stamped on all His words and on the entire tenor of His life. He was bringing men back to God, and He had to remove the obstacles which stood in the way. He had to roll away the stone from the sepulchre in which humanity was entombed and call the dead to come forth. He had to press His weight against the huge iron gates of human guilt and doom and force them open. He had done so; and, as He said, "It is finished," He was at the same time saying to all mankind, "Behold, I have set before you an open door, and no man can shut it."

The more difficult and prolonged any task is, the greater is the satisfaction of finishing it. Everyone knows what it is, after accomplishing anything on which a great deal of labour has been bestowed or the accomplishment of which has been delayed, to be able to say, "There; it is finished at last." In the more signal efforts of human genius and energy there is a satisfaction of final achievement which warms even spectators with sympathy at the distance of hundreds of years. What must it be to the poet, after equipping himself by the labours of a lifetime with the stores of knowledge and the skill in the use of language requisite for the composition of a "Divine Comedy" or a "Paradise Lost," and after wearing himself lean for many years at his task, to be able at last, when the final line has been penned, to write Finis at the bottom of his performance? What must it have been to Columbus, after he had worn his life out in seeking the patronage necessary for his undertaking and endured the perils of voyaging in stormy seas and among mutinous mariners, to see at last the sunlight on the peak of Darien which informed him that his dream was true and his lifework accomplished? When we read how William Wilberforce, the champion of Slave Emancipation, heard on his deathbed, a few hours before he breathed his last, that the British Legislature had agreed to the expenditure necessary to secure the object to which he had sacrificed his life, what heart can refuse its tribute of sympathetic joy, as it thinks of him expiring with the shouts of emancipated millions in his ears? These are feeble suggestions of the triumph with which Christ saw, fallen behind Him, His accomplished task, as He cried, "It is finished."

II.

If Jesus had during life a vast work on hand which He was able on the cross to say He had finished, He was in quite as exceptional a degree a sufferer; yet on the cross He was able to say that His suffering also was finished.

Suffering is the reverse side of work. It is the shadow that accompanies achievement, as his shadow follows a man. It is due to the resistance offered to the worker by the medium in which he toils.

The life of Jesus was one of great suffering, because He had to do His work in an extremely resistant medium. His purpose was so beneficent, and His passion for the good of the world so obvious, that it might have been expected that He would meet with nothing but encouragement and furtherance. He was so religious that all the religious forces might have been expected to second His efforts; He was so patriotic that it would have been natural if His native country had welcomed Him with open arms; He was so philanthropic that He ought to have been the idol of the multitude. But at every step He met with opposition. Everything that was influential in His age and country turned against Him. Obstruction became more and more persistent and cruel, till at length on Calvary it reached its climax, when all the powers of earth and hell were combined with the one purpose of crushing Him and thrusting Him out of existence. And they succeeded.

But the mystery of suffering is very insufficiently explained when it is defined as the reaction of the work on the worker. While a man's work is what he does with the force of his will, suffering is what is done to him against his will. It may be done by the will of opponents and enemies. But this is never the whole explanation. Above this will, which may be thoroughly evil, there is a will which is good and means us good by our suffering.

Suffering is the will of God. It is His chief instrument for fashioning His creatures according to His own plan. While by our work we ought to be seeking to make a bit of the world such as He would have it to be, by our suffering He is seeking to make us such as He would have us to be. He blocks up our pathway by it on this side and on that, in order that we may be kept in the path which He has appointed. He prunes our desires and ambitions; He humbles us and makes us meek and acquiescent. By our work we help to make a well-ordered world, but by our suffering He makes a sanctified man; and in His eyes this is by far the greater triumph.

Perhaps this is the most difficult half of life to manage. While it is by no means easy to accomplish the work of life, it is harder still to bear suffering and to benefit by it. Have you ever seen a man to whom nature had given great talents and grace great virtues, so that the possibilities of his life seemed unbounded, while he had imagination enough to expatiate over them: a man who might have been a missionary, opening up dark countries to civilisation and the gospel; or a statesman, swaying a parliament with his eloquence and shaping the destinies of millions by his wisdom; or a thinker, wrestling with the problems of the age, sowing the seeds of light, and raising for himself an imperishable monument: but who was laid hold of by some remorseless disease or suddenly crushed by some accident; so that all at once his schemes were upset and his life narrowed to petty anxieties about his health and shifts to avoid the evil day, which could not, however, be long postponed? And did it not seem to you, as you watched him, to be far harder for him to accept this destiny with a good grace and with cheerful submission than it would have been to accomplish the career of enterprise and achievement which once seemed to lie before him? To do nothing is often more difficult than to do the greatest things, and to submit requires more faith than to achieve.

The life of Christ was hemmed and crushed in on every hand. Evil men were the proximate cause of this; but He acknowledged behind them the will of God. He had to accept a career of shame instead of glory, of brief and limited activity instead of far-travelling beneficence, of premature and violent death instead of world-wide and everlasting empire. But He never murmured; however bitter any sacrifice might be on other grounds, He made it sweet to Himself by reflecting that it was the will of His Father. When the worst came to the worst, and He was forced to cry, "If it be possible, let this cup pass from Me," He was swift to add, "Nevertheless not My will, but Thine, be done." And thus on step after step of the ladder His thoughts were brought into perfect accord with His Father's, and His will with His Father's will.

At last on the cross the cup out of which He had drunk so often was put into His hands for the last time. The draught was large, black and bitter as never before. But He did not flinch. He drank it up. As He did so, the last segment of the circle of His own perfection completed itself; and, while, flinging the cup away after having exhausted the last drop, He cried, "It is finished," the echo came back from heaven from those who saw with wonder and adoration the perfect round of His completed character, "It is finished."

Though these two sides of the life of Christ are separable in thought, it is evident that they constitute together but one life.[2] The work He did involved the suffering which He bore and lent to it meaning and dignity. On the other hand, the suffering perfected the Worker and thus conferred greatness on His work. In His crowning task of atoning for the sin of the world it was as a sufferer that He accomplished the will of God. And now both are finished; and henceforward the world has a new possession: it has had other perfect things; but never before and never since has it had a perfect life.

[1] "It is finished."

[2] Sometimes they are expressed by saying that life is both a Mission and a Discipline.

CHAPTER XX.

THE SEVENTH WORD FROM THE CROSS[1]

While all the words of dying persons are full of interest, there is special importance attached to the last of them. This is the Last Word of Jesus; and both for this reason and for others it claims particular attention.

A noted Englishman is recorded to have said, when on his deathbed, to a nephew, "Come near and see how a Christian can die." Whether or not that was a wise saying, certainly to learn how to die is one of the most indispensable acquirements of mortals; and nowhere can it be learnt so well as by studying the death of Christ. This Last Word especially teaches us how to die. It will, however, teach us far more, if we have the wit to learn: it contains not only the art of dying but also the art of living.

I.

The final word of the dying Saviour was a prayer. Not all the words from the cross were prayers. One was addressed to the penitent thief, another to His mother and His favourite disciple, and a third to the soldiers who were crucifying Him; but prayer was distinctly the language of His dying hours. It was not by chance that His very last word was a prayer; for the currents within Him were all flowing Godwards.

While prayer is appropriate for all times and seasons, there are occasions when it is singularly appropriate. At the close of the day, when we are about to enter into the state of sleep, which is an image of death, the most natural of all states of mind is surely prayer. In moments of mortal peril, as on shipboard when a multitude are suddenly confronted with death, an irresistible impulse presses men to their knees. At the communion table, when the bread and the wine are circulating in silence, every thoughtful person is inevitably occupied with prayer. But on a death-bed it is more in its place than anywhere else. Then we are perforce parting with all that is earthly—with relatives and friends, with business and property, with the comforts of home and the face of the earth. How natural to lay hold of what alone we can keep hold of; and this is what prayer does; for it lays hold of God.

It is so natural to pray then that prayer might be supposed to be an invariable element of the last scenes. But it is not always. A death-bed without God is an awful sight; yet it does occur. The currents of the mind may be flowing so powerfully earthward that even then they cannot be diverted. There are even death-beds where the thought of God is a terror which the dying man keeps away; and sometimes his friends assist him to keep it away, suffering none to be seen and nothing to be said that could call God to mind. Natural as prayer is, it is only so to those who have learned to pray before. It had long been to Jesus the language of life. He had prayed without ceasing—on the mountain-top and in the busy haunts of men, by Himself and in company with others—and it was only the bias of the life asserting itself in death when, as He breathed His last, He turned to God.

If, then, we would desire our last words to be words of prayer, we should commence to pray at once. If the face of God is to shine on our death-bed, we must now acquaint ourselves with Him and be at peace. If, as we look upon the dying Christ or on the dying saints, we say, "Let me die the death of the righteous, and let my last end be like his," then we must begin now to live the life of the righteous and to practise its gracious habits.

II.

The last word of the dying Saviour was a quotation from Scripture.

This was not the first time our Lord quoted Scripture on the cross: His great cry, "My God, My God, why hast Thou forsaken Me?" was likewise borrowed from the Old Testament, and it is possible that there is Scriptural allusion in others of the Seven Words.

If prayer is natural to the lips of the dying, so is Scripture. For different seasons and for different uses there is special suitability in different languages and literatures. Latin is the language of law and scholarship, French of conversation and diplomacy, German of philosophy, English of commerce. But in the most sacred moments and transactions of life there is no language like that of the Bible. Especially is this the case in everything connected with death. On a tombstone, for example, how irrelevant, as a rule, seem all other quotations, but how perfect is the fitness of a verse from Scripture. And on a death-bed there are no words which so well become the dying lips.

This is strikingly illustrated by the following extract, guaranteed as authentic, from a private diary:—"I remember, when I was a student, visiting a dying man. He had been in the university with me, but a few years ahead; and, at the close of a brilliant career in college, he was appointed to a professorship of philosophy in a colonial university. But, after a very few years, he fell into bad health; and he came home to Scotland to die. It was a summer Sunday afternoon when I called to see him, and it happened that I was able to offer him a drive. His great frame was with difficulty got into the open carriage; but then he lay back comfortably and was able to enjoy the fresh air. Two other friends were with him that day—college companions, who had come out from the city to visit him. On the way back they dropped into the rear, and I was alone beside him, when he began to talk with appreciation of their friendship and kindness. 'But,' he said, 'do you know what they have been doing all day?' I could not guess. 'Well,' he said, 'they have been reading to me *Sartor Resartus*; and oh! I am awfully tired of it.' Then, turning on me his large eyes, he began to repeat, 'This is a faithful saying, and worthy of all acceptation, that Jesus Christ came into the world to save sinners, of whom I am chief;' and then he added with great earnestness, 'There is nothing else of any use to me now.' I had not opened the subject at all: perhaps I was afraid to introduce it to one whom I felt to be so much my superior; but I need not say how overjoyed I was to obtain such a glimpse into the very depths of a great, true mind." *Sartor Resartus* is one of the best of books; there are few to be so heartily recommended. Yet there are moments in life—and those immediately before death are among them—when even such a book may be felt to be irrelevant, and, indeed, no book is appropriate except the one which contains the words of eternal life.

It is worth noting from which portion of the Old Testament Jesus fetched the word on which He stayed up His soul in this supreme moment. The quotation is from the thirty-first Psalm. The other great word uttered on the cross to which I have already alluded was also taken from one of the Psalms—the twenty-second. This is undoubtedly the most precious of all the books of the Old Testament. It is a book penned as with the life-blood of its authors; it is the record of humanity's profoundest sorrows and sublimest ecstasies; it is the most perfect expression which has ever been given to experience; it has been the *vade-mecum* of all the saints; and to know and love it is one of the best signs of spirituality.

Jesus knew where to go in the Bible for the language that suited Him; for He had been a diligent student of it all His days. He heard it in the home of His childhood; He listened to it in the synagogue; probably He got the use of the synagogue rolls and hung over it in secret. He knew it through and through. Therefore, when He became a preacher, His language was saturated with it, and in controversy, by the apt use of it, He could put to shame those who were its professional students. But in His private life likewise He employed it in every exigency. He fought with it the enemy in the wilderness and overcame him; and now, in the supreme need of a dying hour, it stood Him in good stead. It is to those who, like Jesus, have hidden God's Word in their hearts that it is a present help in every time of need; and, if we wish to stay ourselves upon it in dying, we ought to make it the man of our counsel in living.

It is worth observing in what manner Jesus made this quotation from the Psalter: He added something at the beginning and He omitted something at the close. At the beginning He added, "Father." This is not in the psalm. It could not have been. In the Old Testament the individual had not begun yet to address God by this name, though God was called the Father of the nation as a whole. The new consciousness of God which Christ introduced into the world is embodied in this word, and, by prefixing it to the citation, He gave the verse a new colouring. We may, then, do this with the Old Testament: we may put New-Testament meaning into it. Indeed, in connection with this very verse we have a still more remarkable illustration of the same treatment. Stephen, the first martyr of Christianity, was in many respects very like his Master, and in his martyrdom closely imitated Him. Thus on the field of death he repeated Christ's prayer for His enemies—"Lord, lay not this sin to their charge." Also, he imitated this final word, but he put it in a new form, "Lord Jesus, receive my spirit;" that is, he addressed to Christ the dying prayer which Christ Himself addressed to the Father.[2] The other alteration which Jesus made was the omission of the words, "for Thou hast redeemed me." It would not have been fitting for Him to employ them. But we will not omit them; and if, like Stephen, we address the prayer to Christ, how much richer and more pathetic are the words to us than they were even to him who first penned them.

III.

It was about His spirit that the dying Saviour prayed.

Dying persons are sometimes much taken up with their bodies. Their pain and trouble may occasion this, and the prescriptions of the physician may require close attention. Some display a peculiar anxiety even about what is to happen to the body after the life has left it, giving the minutest instructions as to their own obsequies. Not infrequently the minds of the dying are painfully occupied with their worldly affairs: they have their property to dispose of, and they are distracted with anxieties about their families. The example of Jesus shows that it is not wrong to bestow attention on these things even on a deathbed; for His fifth word, "I thirst," had reference to His own bodily necessities; and, whilst hanging on the cross, He made provision for His mother's future comfort. But His supreme concern was His spirit; to the interests of which He devoted His final prayer.

What is the spirit? It is the finest, highest, sacredest part of our being. In modern and ordinary language we call it the soul, when we speak of man as composed of body and soul; but in the language of Scripture it is distinguished even from the soul as the most lofty and exquisite part of the inner man. It is to the rest of our nature what the flower is to the plant or what the pearl is to the shell. It is that within us which is specially allied to God and eternity. It is also, however, that which sin seeks to corrupt and our spiritual enemies seek to destroy. No doubt these are specially active in the article of death; it is their last chance; and fain would they seize the spirit as it parts from the body and, dragging it down, rob it of its destiny. Jesus knew that He was launching out into eternity; and, plucking His spirit away from these hostile hands which were eager to seize it, He placed it in the hands of God. There it was safe. Strong and secure are the hands of the Eternal. They are soft and loving too. With what a passion of tenderness must they have received the spirit of Jesus. "I have covered thee," said God to His servant in an ancient prophecy, "in the shadow of My hand;" and now Jesus, escaping from all the enemies, visible and invisible, by whom He was beset, sought the fulfilment of this prophecy.

This is the art of dying; but is it not also the art of living? The spirit of every son of Adam is threatened by dangers at death; but it is threatened with them also in life. As has been said, it is our flower and our pearl; but the flower may be crushed and the pearl may be lost long before death arrives. "The flesh lusteth against the spirit." So does the world. Temptation assails it, sin denies it. No better prayer, therefore, could be offered by a living man, morning by morning, than this of the dying Saviour. Happy is he who can say, in reference to his spirit, "I know whom I have believed, and I am persuaded that He is able to keep that which I have committed to Him against that day."

IV.

This last word of the expiring Saviour revealed His view of death.

The word used by Jesus in commending His spirit to God implies that He was giving it away in the hope of finding it again. He was making a deposit in a safe place, to which, after the crisis of death was over, He would come and recover it. Such is the force of the word, as is easily seen in the quotation just made from St. Paul, where he says that he knows that God will keep that which he has committed to Him—using the same word as Jesus—"against that day." [3] Which day? Obviously some point in the future when he could appear and claim from God that which he had entrusted to Him. Such a date was also in Christ's eye when He said, "Father, into Thy hands I commend my spirit." Death is a disruption of the parts of which human nature is composed. One part—the spirit—was going away to God; another was in the hands of men, who were wreaking on it their wicked will; and it was on its way to the house appointed for all living. But Jesus was looking forward to a reunion of the separated parts, when they would again find each other, and the integrity of the personal life be restored.

The most momentous question which the dying can ask, or which the living can ask in the prospect of death, is, "If a man die, shall he live again?" does he all die? and does he die forever? There is a terrible doubt in the human heart that it may be so; and there have never been wanting teachers who have turned this doubt into a dogma. They hold that mind is only a form or a function of matter, and that, therefore, in the dissolution of the bodily materials, man dissolves and mixes with the material universe. Others, while holding fast the distinction between mind and matter, have taught that, as the body returns to the dust, the mind returns to the ocean of being, in which its personality is lost, as the drop is in the sea, and there can be no reunion. There is, however, something high and sacred within us that rebels against these doctrines; and the best teachers of the race have encouraged us to hope for something better. Still, their assurances have been hesitating and their own faith obscure. It is to Christ we have to go: He has the words of eternal life. He spoke on this subject without hesitation or obscurity; and His dying word proves that He believed for Himself what He taught to others. Not only, however, has He by His teaching brought life and immortality to light: He is Himself the guarantee of the doctrine; for He is our immortal life. Because we are united to Him we know we can never perish; nothing, not even death, can separate us from His love; "Because I live," He has said, "ye shall live also."

It may be that in a very literal sense we have in the study of this sentence been learning the art of dying: these may be our own dying words. They have been the dying words of many. When John Huss was being led to execution, there was stuck on his head a paper cap, scrawled over with pictures of devils, to whom the wretched priests by whom he was surrounded consigned his soul; but again and again he cried, "Father, into Thy hands I commend my spirit." These were also the last words of Polycarp, of Jerome of Prague, of Luther, of Melanchthon, and of many others. Who could wish his spirit to be carried away to God in a more glorious vehicle? But, whether or not we may use this prayer in death, let us diligently make use of it in life. Close not the book without breathing, "Father, into Thy hands I commend my spirit."

[1] "Father, into Thy hands I commend My spirit."

[2] The first business of the interpreter of Scripture is to find out precisely what every verse or paragraph meant at the time and place where it was written; and there is endless profit in the exact determination of this original application. But, whilst the interpreter's task begins, it does not end with this. The Bible is a book for every generation; and the deduction of the message which it is intended to convey to the present day is as truly the task of the interpreter. There is a species of exegesis, sometimes arrogating to itself the sole title to be considered scientific, by which the garden of Scripture is transmuted into an herbarium of withered specimens.

[3] Christ's word is *paratithemai*, and St. Paul's, 2 Tim. i. 12, *ten paratheken mou*, according to the best reading.

CHAPTER XXI.

THE SIGNS

There are indications that to some of those who took part in the crucifixion of Christ His death presented hardly anything to distinguish it from an ordinary execution; and there were others who were anxious to believe that it had no features which were extraordinary. But God did not leave His Son altogether without witness. The end of the Saviour's sufferings was accompanied by certain signs, which showed the interest excited by them in the world unseen.

I.

The first sign was the rending of the veil of the temple. This was a heavy curtain covering the entrance to the Holy Place or the entrance to the Holy of Holies—most probably the latter. Both entrances were thus protected, and Josephus gives the following description of one of the curtains, which will probably convey a fair idea of either; five ells high and sixteen broad, of Babylonian texture, and wonderfully stitched of blue, white, scarlet and purple—representing the universe in its four elements—scarlet standing for fire and blue for air by their colours, and the white linen for earth and the purple for sea on account of their derivation, the one, from the flax of the earth and the other from the shellfish of the sea.

The fact that the rent proceeded from top to bottom was considered to indicate that it was made by the finger of God; but whether any physical means may have been employed we cannot tell. Some have thought of the earthquake, which took place at the same moment, as being connected with it through the loosening of a beam or some similar accident.[1]

At critical moments in history, when the minds of men are charged with excitement, even slight accidents may assume remarkable significance.[2] Such incidents occur at turning-points of the life even of individuals.[3] They derive their significance from the emotion with which the minds of observers happen at the time to be filled. No doubt the rending of the temple veil might appear to some a pure accident, while in the minds of others it crystallised a hundred surging thoughts. But we must ascribe to it a higher dignity and a divine intention.

Like the pillar of cloud and fire in the wilderness, it had a double face—one of judgment and another of mercy.

It betokened the desecration of the shrine and the exodus of the Deity from the temple whose day of opportunity and usefulness was over. And it is curious to note how at the time not only the Christian but even the Jewish mind was big with this thought. There is a Jewish legend in Josephus, which is referred to also by the Roman historian Tacitus, that at the Passover some years after this the east door of the inner court of the temple, which was so heavy that twenty men were required to close it, and was, besides, at the moment strongly locked and barred, suddenly at midnight flew open; and, the following Pentecost, the priests whose duty it was to guard the court by night, heard first a rushing noise as of hurrying feet and then a loud cry, as of many voices, saying, "Let us depart from hence."

Nor was it only in Palestine that in that age the air was charged with the impression that a turning-point in history had been reached, and that the ancient world was passing away. Plutarch[4] heard a singular story of one Epitherses from the rhetorician Aemilianus, who had it from the man's father. On a certain occasion this Epitherses happened to be a passenger on board a ship which got becalmed among the Echinades. As it stood near one of the islands, suddenly there came from the shore a voice, loud and clear, calling Thamus, the pilot, an Egyptian, by his name. Twice he kept silence; but, when the call came the third time, he replied; whereupon the voice cried still louder, "When you come to the Paludes, proclaim that the great Pan is dead." Pan being the god of nature in that ancient world, all who heard were terrified, and they debated whether or not they should obey the command. At last it was agreed that if, when they came to the Paludes, it was windy, they were not to obey, but, if calm, they would. It turned out to be calm; and, accordingly, the pilot, standing on the prow of the vessel, shouted out the words; whereupon the air was filled, not with an echo, but the loud groaning of a great multitude mingled with surprise.[5] The pilot was called before the Emperor Tiberius, who strictly enquired into the truth of the incident.

Such was the meaning of the rending of the veil on its dark side: it denoted that the reign of the gods was over and that Jerusalem was no longer to be the place where men ought to worship. But it had at the same time a bright side; and this was the side for the sake of which the incident was treasured by the friends of Jesus. It meant, as St. Paul says, that the wall between Jew and Gentile had been broken down. It meant, as is set forth in the noble argument of the Epistle to the Hebrews, that the system of ceremonies and intermediaries by which under the Old Testament the worshipper might approach God and yet was kept at a distance from Him had been swept away. The heart of God is now fully revealed, and it is a heart of love; and, at the same time, the heart of man, liberated by the sacrifice of Christ from the conscience of sin, as it could never be by the offering of bulls and goats, can joyfully venture into the divine presence and go out and in with the freedom of a child. "Having therefore, brethren, boldness to enter into the holiest by the blood of Jesus, by a new and living way, which He hath consecrated for us, through the veil—that is to say, His flesh—and having a High Priest over the house of God, let us draw near with a true heart in full assurance of faith." [6]

II.

The second sign was the resurrection of certain of the dead—"The graves were opened, and many bodies of the saints which slept arose and came out of the graves after His resurrection, and went into the holy city and appeared unto many."

Whether or not the rending of the veil in the temple was connected with the earthquake, there is no doubt that this second sign was. The graves in Palestine were caves in the rocks, the mouths of which were closed with great stones. Some of these stones were shaken from their places by the earthquake; and the bodies themselves, which lay on shelves or stood upright in niches, may have been disturbed. But in some of them a greater disturbance occurred: besides the external shaking there took place within them a motion of the life-giving breath of God.

In the minds of many devout scholars this miracle has excited suspicion on several accounts. They say it is contrary to the teaching of Scripture elsewhere, according to which Christ was the firstfruits of them that slept. If these dead bodies were reanimated at the moment of this earthquake, they, and not He, were the firstfruits. To this it is answered that St. Matthew is careful to note that they came out of their graves "after His resurrection"; so that St. Matthew still agrees with St. Paul in making Christ the first to rise. But, then, it is asked, in what condition were they between their reanimation and their resurrection? The Evangelist appears to state that they rose from death to life at the moment of the earthquake, but did not emerge from the tomb till the third day afterwards, when Christ had risen. Is this credible? or is it an apocryphal marvel, which has been interpolated in the text of St. Matthew? The other Evangelists, while, along with St. Matthew, narrating the rending of the veil, do not touch on this incident at all. The whole representation, it is argued, lacks the sobriety which is characteristic of the authentic miracles of the Gospels and broadly separates them from the ecclesiastical miracles, about which there is generally an air of triviality and grotesqueness.

On the other hand, there is no indication in the oldest and best manuscripts of St. Matthew that this is an interpolation; and many of the acutest minds have felt this trait to be thoroughly congruous and suitable to its place. If, they contend, He who had just died on Calvary was what He gave Himself out and we believe Him to be, His death must have excited the profoundest commotion in the kingdoms of the dead. The world of living men and women was insensible to the character of the event which was taking place before its eyes; but the world unseen was agitated as it never had been before and never was to be again. It was not unnatural, but the reverse, that some of the dead, in their excitement and eagerness, should even press back over the boundaries of the other world, in order to be in the world where Christ was. The question where they were or what they were doing between their reanimation and resurrection is a triviality not worth considering. At all events, they rose after their Lord; and was it not appropriate that when, after the forty days, He ascended to heaven, there to be received by rejoicing angels and archangels, He should not only appear in the flesh, but be accompanied by specimens of what His resurrection power was ultimately to do for all believers? If it be asked who the favoured saints were to whom this blessed priority was vouchsafed, we cannot tell. The dust, however, was not far away of many whom the Lord might delight to honour—patriarchs, like Abraham; kings, like David; prophets, like Isaiah.

But the true significance of this sign is not dependent on such speculations. Even if it should ever be discovered, as it is not in the least likely to be, that this story was interpolated in St. Matthew, and we should be driven to the conclusion that it was invented by the excited fancy of the primitive Christians, even then we should have to ask what caused them to invent it. And the only possible answer would be, that it was the force of the conviction burning within them that by His death and resurrection Christ had opened the gates of death to all the saints. This was the glorious faith which was begotten by the experiences of those never-to-be-forgotten days, whether the sight of these resurrected saints played any part or not in maturing it; and it is now the faith of the Church and the faith of mankind.

This may well be called the rending of another veil. If in the ancient world there was a veil on the face of God, there was a veil likewise on the face of eternity.[7] The home of the soul was hidden from the children of men. They vaguely surmised it, indeed; they could never believe that they were wholly dust. But, apart from Christ, the speculations even of the wisest as to the other world are hardly more correct or certain than might be the speculations of infants in the womb as to the condition of this world.[8] Christ, on the contrary, always spoke of the world invisible with the freedom and confidence of one to whom it was native and well known; and His resurrection and ascension afford the most authentic glimpses into the realm of immortality which the world has ever received.

In this sign, indeed, it is with the death and not with the resurrection that this authentication is connected. But the resurrection of Christ is allied in the most intimate manner with His death. It was the public recognition of His righteousness. Since, however, He died not for Himself alone, but as a public person, His mystical body has the same right to resurrection, and in due time it will be made manifest that, He having discharged every claim on their behalf, death has now no right to detain them.

III.

The first sign was in the physical world; the second was in the underworld of the dead; but the third was in the common world of living men. This was the acknowledgment of Christ by the centurion who superintended His crucifixion.

Whether, like the preceding signs, this third one is to be connected with the earthquake is a question. Probably the answer ought to be in the affirmative. The sensation produced by an earthquake is like nothing else in nature; and its first effect on an unsophisticated mind is to create the sense that God is near. Probably, therefore, the earthquake was felt by the centurion to be the divine Amen to the thoughts which had been rising in his mind, and it gave them a speedy and complete delivery in his confession.

This confession was, however, the result of his observation of Jesus throughout His whole trial and the subsequent proceedings; and it is an eloquent tribute to our Lord's behaviour. The centurion may have been at the side of Jesus from the arrest to the end. Through those unparalleled hours he had observed the rage and injustice of His enemies; and he had marked how patient, unretaliating, gentle and magnanimous He had been. He had heard Him praying for His crucifiers, comforting the thief on the cross, providing for His mother, communing with God. More and more his interest was excited and his heart stirred, till at last he was standing opposite the cross,[9] drinking in every syllable and devouring every movement; and, when the final prayer was uttered and the earthquake answered it, his rising conviction brimmed over and he could not withhold his testimony.

St. Luke makes him say only, "This was a righteous man," while the others report, "This was the Son of God." But St. Luke's may include theirs; because, if the centurion meant to state that the claims of Jesus were just, what were His claims? At Pilate's judgment-seat he had heard it stated that Jesus claimed to be the Son of God, and perhaps he had heard Him make this claim Himself in reply to Pilate's question. This name, along with others like it, had been hurled at Jesus, in his hearing, by those standing round the cross.

But what did he mean when he made this acknowledgment? It has been held that all which he, a heathen, could imply was that Jesus was a son of God in the sense in which the Greeks and Romans believed Hercules, Castor and other heroes to be sons of their deities. This may be near the truth; but his soul was moved, his mind was opened; and, once in the way, he could easily proceed further in the knowledge of Christ. Tradition says that his name was Longinus, and that he became bishop of Cappadocia and ultimately died a martyr.

Have we not here the rending of a third veil? There is a veil on the face of God which requires to be removed; and there is a veil on the face of eternity which requires to be removed; but the most fatal veil is that which is on the heart of the individual and prevents him from seeing the glory of Christ. It was on the faces of nearly all the multitude that day assembled round the cross. It was on the faces of the poor soldiers gambling within a few feet of the dying Saviour; in their case it was a veil of insensibility. It was on the faces of the ecclesiastics and the mob of Jerusalem; and in their case it was a thick veil of prejudice. The greatest sight ever witnessed on earth was there beside them; but they were stoneblind to it.

The glory of Christ is still the greatest sight which anyone can see between the cradle and the grave. And it is now as near everyone of us as it was to the crowd on Calvary. Some see it; for the veil upon their faces is rent; and they are transfixed and transformed by the sight. But others are blinded. How near one may be to Jesus, how much mixed up with His cause, how well informed about His life and doctrine, and yet never see His glory or know Him as a personal Saviour! It is said that people may spend a lifetime in the midst of perfect scenery and yet never awake to its charm; but by comes a painter or poet and drinks the beauty in, till he is intoxicated with it and puts it into a glorious picture or a deathless song. So can some remember a time when Jesus, though in a sense well known, was nothing to them; but at a certain point a veil seemed to rend and an entire change supervened; and ever since then the world is full of Him; His name seems written on the stars and among the flowers; He is their first thought when they wake and their last before they sleep; He is with them in the house and by the way; He is their all in all.

This is the most critical rending of the veil; because, when it takes place, the others follow. When we have our eyes opened to see the glory of Christ, we soon know the Father also; and the darkness passes from the face of eternity, because eternity for us is to be forever with the Lord.

[1] "May this phenomenon account for the early conversion of so many priests recorded in Acts vi. 7?"—EDERSHEIM.

[2] Shakespeare is very fond of describing the portents by which remarkable events are foreshadowed. Thus, *Julius Caesar*, Act I. Scene ii.:—

    "O Cicero,
I have seen tempests, when the scolding winds
Have rived the knotty oaks; and I have seen
Th' ambitious ocean swell and rage and foam,
To be exalted with the threatening clouds;
But never till to-night, never till now
Did I go through a tempest dropping fire.
A common slave—you know him well by sight—

Held up his left hand, which did flame and burn
Like twenty torches joined; and yet his hand,
Not sensible of fire, remained unscorched.
Besides—I ha' not since put up my sword—
Against the Capitol I met a lion,
Who glared upon me and went surly by,
Without annoying me. And there were drawn
Upon a heap an hundred ghastly women,
Transformed with their fear, who swore they saw
Men, all in fire, walk up and down the streets.
And yesterday the bird of night did sit
Even at noonday upon the marketplace,
Hooting and shrieking. When these prodigies
Do so conjointly meet, let not men say,
'These are their reasons—they are natural,'
For I believe they are portentous things
Unto the climate that they point upon."

See also Act II., Scene ii., and Act V., Scene i. of the same play; *Macbeth*, Act II., Scene ii.; *Hamlet*, Act I., Scene i. Such impressions are not, however, even in modern times, confined to poetry alone. Historical instances will suggest themselves to every reader.

[3] Some of the most interesting I have read occur in a brief memoir of the founder of the Bagster Publishing Company issued on the centenary of its opening.

[4] *De Oraculorum Defectu*, quoted by Heubner in his commentary, *in loc*.

[5] *stenagmos ama thaumasmo*.

[6] Heb. x. 19-22.

[7] So the ignorance of immortality is expressly called in the beautiful passage, Isa. xxv. 7.

[8] Sir Thomas Browne, *Hydrotaphia*, chap. iv.: "A dialogue between two infants in the womb concerning the state of this world might handsomely illustrate our ignorance of the next, where, methinks, we still discourse in Plato's den, and are but embryo philosophers."

[9] *Parestekos ex enantias autou.*

CHAPTER XXII.

THE DEAD CHRIST

It was not usual to remove bodies from the cross immediately after their death. They were allowed to hang, exposed to the weather, till they rotted and fell to pieces; or they might be torn by birds or beasts; and at last a fire was perhaps kindled beneath the cross to rid the place of the remains. Such was the Roman custom; but among the Jews there was more scrupulosity. In their law there stood this provision: "If a man have committed a sin worthy of death, and he be put to death, and thou hang him on a tree, his body shall not remain all night upon the tree, but thou shalt in any wise bury him that day (for he that is hanged is accursed of God); that thy land be not defiled which the Lord thy God giveth thee for an inheritance." [1] Whether or not the Jews always tried to get this provision observed in executions carried out in their midst by their Roman masters, we cannot tell; but it was natural that they should do so in reference to executions carried out in the neighbourhood of the holy city and at Passover time. In the present instance there was the additional reason, that the morrow of the execution of Jesus was a high day—it was the Sabbath of the Passover—a kind of double Sabbath, which would have been desecrated by any unclean thing, like an unburied corpse, exposed to view. The Jews were extremely sensitive about such points. At any time they regarded themselves as unclean if they touched a dead body, and they had to go through a process of purgation before their sense of sanctity was restored. But on the occasion of a Passover Sabbath they would have felt it to be a desecration if any dead thing had even met their eyes or rested uncovered on the soil of their city. Therefore their representatives went to the Roman governor and begged that the three crucified men should be put to death by clubbing and their bodies buried before the Sabbath commenced.

The suggestion has often been made that, behind this pretended scrupulosity, their real aim was to inflict additional pain and indignity on Jesus. The breaking of the bones of the body, by smashing them with clubs, was a peculiarly horrible form of punishment sometimes inflicted by the Romans.[2] It was nearly as cruel and degrading as crucifixion itself; and it was an independent punishment, not conjoined with crucifixion. But the Jews in this case attempted to get them united, that Jesus, besides being crucified, might, so to speak, die yet another death of the most revolting description. The Evangelist, however, throws no doubt on the motive which they put forward—namely, that the Passover Sabbath might be saved from desecration—and, although their insatiable hatred may have made them suggest clubbing as the mode by which His death should be hastened, we need not question that their scruples were genuine. It is an extraordinary instance of the game of self-deception which the human conscience can play. Here were people fresh from the greatest crime ever committed—their hands still reeking, one might say, with the blood of the Innocent—and their consciences, while utterly untouched with remorse for this crime, are anxious about the observance of the Sabbath and the ceremonial defilement of the soil. It is the most extraordinary illustration which history records of how zeal for what may be called the body of religion may be utterly destitute of any connection with its spirit. It is surely a solemn warning to make sure that every outward religious act is accompanied by the genuine outgoing of the heart to God, and a warning that, if we love not our brother, whom we have seen, neither can we be lovers of God, whom we have not seen.

Pilate hearkened to the request of the Jews, and orders were given to the soldiers to act accordingly. Then the ghastly work began. They broke the legs of the malefactor on the one side of Jesus, and then those of the other on the opposite side. The penitent thief was not spared; but what a difference his penitence made! To his companion this was nothing but an additional indignity; to him it was the knocking-off of the fetters, that his spirit might the sooner wing its way to Paradise, where Christ had trysted to meet him.

Then came the turn of Jesus. But, when the soldiers looked at Him, they saw that their work was unnecessary: death had been before them; the drooping head and pallid frame were those of a dead man. Only, to make assurance doubly sure, one of them thrust his spear into the body, making a wound so large that Jesus, when He was risen, could invite the doubting Thomas to thrust his hand into it; and, as the weapon was drawn forth again, there came out after it blood and water.

St. John, who was on the spot and saw all this taking place, seems to have perceived in the scene an unusual importance; for he adds to his report these words of confirmation, as if he were sealing an official document, "And he that saw it bare record; and his record is true; and he knoweth that he saith true, that ye might believe." Why should he interrupt the flow of his narrative to add these words of assurance?

Some have thought that he was moved to do so by a heresy which sprang up in the early Church to the effect that Christ was not really human: His body, it was said, was only a phantom body, and therefore His death was only an apparent death. In opposition to such a notion St. John directs attention to the realistic details, which prove so conclusively that this was a real man and that He died a real death. Of course that ancient heresy has long ceased to trouble; there are none now who deny that Jesus was a man. Yet it is curious how the tendency ever and anon reappears to evaporate the facts of His life. At the present hour there are eminent Christian teachers in Europe who are treating the resurrection of the Lord in very much the same way as these early

Docetae treated His death—as a kind of figure of speech, not to be understood too literally. Against such the Church must lift up the crude facts of the resurrection as St. John did those of the death of the Saviour.[3] In our generation teachers of every kind are appealing to Christ and putting Him in the centre of theology; but we must ask them, What Christ? Is it the Christ of the Scriptures: the Christ who in the beginning was with God; who was incarnated; who died for the sins of the world; who was raised from the dead and reigns for evermore? We must not delude ourselves with words: only the Christ of the Scriptures could have brought us the salvation of the Scriptures.

What excited the wonder of St. John is supposed by others to have been the fulfilment of two passages of the Old Testament Scripture which he quotes. It appeared to be a matter of mere chance that the soldiers, contrary to the intention of the Jews, refrained from breaking the bones of Jesus; yet a sacred word, of which they knew nothing, written hundreds of years before, had said, "A bone of Him shall not be broken." It seemed the most casual circumstance that the soldier plunged the spear into the side of Jesus, to make sure that He was dead; yet an ancient oracle, of which he knew nothing, had said, "They shall look on Him whom they pierced." Thus, by the overruling providence of God, the soldiers, going with rude unconcern about their work, were unconsciously fulfilling the Scriptures; and those who both saw what they had done and knew the Scriptures recognised the Divine finger pointing out Jesus as the Sent of God.

The first of these texts is generally supposed[4] to be taken from the account in Exodus of the institution of the Passover, and originally it refers to the paschal lamb, which was to be eaten whole, the breaking of its bones being forbidden. St. John's idea is that Christ was to be the paschal lamb of the New Dispensation, and that therefore Providence took care that nothing should be done to destroy His resemblance to the type, as would have happened if His bones had been broken. The Passover was the great event of the year in all the generations of Jewish history. It was intended to carry the minds of God's people back to the wonderful scenes of divine grace and power in which their existence as a nation had begun, when God liberated them from their bondage and led them out of Egypt with a mighty hand. The centre of the solemnity was the slaying and eating of the paschal lamb. This reminded them of how in Egypt the blood of this lamb, sprinkled on the lintels and doorposts of their huts, saved them from the visit of the destroying angel, who was passing through the land; and how, at the same time, the flesh of the lamb was eaten by the people, with their loins girt and staves in their hands, and supplied them with strength for their adventurous journey. Thus through all ages it impressed on them two things—that the sins of the past required to be expiated, and that strength had to be obtained from above for the new stage of their history on which at the annual Passover they might be supposed to be entering. In the same way, in the New Dispensation, are our minds ever to revert to the marvellous revelation of the grace and saving power of God in which Christianity originated; and in the very midst is the Lamb slain, who is both the expiation of the sins that are past and the strength requisite for the conflict and the pilgrimage. "If we walk in the light, as He is in the light, we have fellowship one with another, and the blood of Jesus Christ His Son cleanseth us from all sin."

The other words of prophecy which appeared to St. John to be fulfilled on this occasion were, "They shall look on Him whom they pierced." They are from a passage in Zechariah, which is so remarkable that it may be quoted in full—"And I will pour out on the house of David and upon the inhabitants of Jerusalem the spirit of grace and of supplications, and they shall look upon Me whom they have pierced, and they shall mourn for Him, as one mourneth for his only son, and shall be in bitterness for Him, as one that is in bitterness for his firstborn." Jehovah speaks figuratively of the opposition shown to Himself and His servants as piercing Him with pain, just as we say of an insult that it cuts to the heart. But in the death of Jesus the figure became a fact: against the sacred person of the Son of God the spear was lifted up, and it was driven home without compunction. Evidently St. John thinks of this rather as the act of the Jewish people than of the Roman soldier. But the prophecy speaks not only of the people piercing God, but of their looking at their own work with shame and tears. At Pentecost this began to be fulfilled; and in every age since there have been members of the Jewish race who have acknowledged their guilt in the transaction. The full acknowledgment, however, still lingers; but the conversion of God's ancient people, when it comes, must begin with this. Indeed, every human being to whom his own true relation to Christ is revealed must make the same acknowledgment. It was the heart not of a few soldiers or of the representatives of a single people, but of the human race, that hardened itself against Him. It was the sin of the world that nailed Him to the tree and shed His blood. Every sinner may therefore feel that he had a hand in it; and it is only when we see our own sin as aiming at the very existence of God in the death of His Son that we comprehend it in all its enormity.

There have been many who have found the reason for St. John's wonder in the fact that out of the wounded side there flowed blood and water.

From a corpse, when it is pierced—at least, if it has been some time dead—it is not usual for anything to flow. But whether St. John reflected on this or not we cannot tell. What fascinated him was simply the fact that the piercing of the body of the Saviour made it a fountain out of which sprang this double outflow. When the rock in the wilderness was smitten with the rod of Moses, there issued from it a stream which was life to the perishing multitude; but in the double stream coming from the side of Jesus St. John saw something better even than that; because to him the blood symbolized the atonement, and the water the Spirit of Christ; and in these two all our salvation lies.[5] So we sing in the most precious of all our hymns,—

> Let the water and the blood
> From Thy living side which flowed
> Be of sin the double cure—
> Cleanse me from its guilt and power.

Although, however, St. John did not perhaps speculate on the reason why this double outflow took place from the wounded side, others have occupied themselves with the question.

Some[6] have considered the phenomenon altogether abnormal, and endeavoured to explain it from the peculiarity of our Lord's humanity. Though He died. He was not, like other men, to see corruption; His body was to escape in a few hours, transfigured and glorious, from the grasp of death. This transforming process, which issued in His resurrection, began as soon as He was dead; and the spear-thrust, breaking in on it, so to speak, revealed something altogether unique in the constitution of His body.

Others, keeping within the limits of ascertained fact, have given a totally different yet a peculiarly interesting explanation. They have directed attention to the suddenness of Christ's death. It was usual for crucified persons to linger for days; but He did not survive more than six hours. Yet immediately before dying He again and again cried with a loud voice, as if His bodily force were by no means exhausted. Suddenly, however, with a loud cry His life terminated. To what could this be due? It is said that sometimes, under the pressure of intense mental and physical agony, the heart bursts; there is a shriek, and of course death is instantaneous. We speak of people dying of a broken heart—using the phrase only figuratively—but sometimes it can be used literally: the heart is actually ruptured with grief. Now, it is said that, when this takes place, the blood contained in the heart is poured into a sac by which it is surrounded; and there it separates into two substances—a clotty substance of the colour of blood and a pure, colourless substance like water. And, if the sac, when in this condition, were pierced by a spear or any other instrument, there would flow out a large quantity of both substances, which would by an unscientific spectator be described as blood and water.

It was by an English medical man that this theory was first propounded fifty years ago,[7] and it has been adopted by other medical men, equally famous for their scientific eminence and Christian character, such as the late Professor Begbie and Sir James Simpson. The latter well brings out the point and the pathos of this view of the Saviour's death in these words:[8] "It has always appeared—to my medical mind at least—that this view of the mode by which death was produced in the human body of Christ intensifies all our thoughts and ideas regarding the immensity of the sacrifice which He made for our sinful race upon the cross. Nothing can be more striking and startling than the passiveness with which, for our sakes, God as man submitted His incarnate body to the horrors and tortures of the crucifixion. But our wonderment at the stupendous sacrifice increases when we reflect that, whilst thus enduring for our sins the most cruel and agonising form of corporeal death, He was ultimately slain, not by the effects of the anguish of His corporeal frame, but by the effects of the mightier anguish of His mind; the fleshly walls of His heart—like the veil, as it were, in the temple of His body—becoming rent and riven, as for us He poured out His soul unto death—the travail of His soul in that awful hour thus standing out as unspeakably more bitter and dreadful than even the travail of His body."

In this chapter we have been moving somewhat in the region of speculation and conjecture, and we have not rigidly ascertained what is logically tenable and what is not. This is a place of mystery, where dim yet imposing meanings peep out on us in whatever direction we turn. We have called the scene the Dead Christ. But who does not see that the dead Christ is so interesting and wonderful because He is also the living Christ? He lives; He is here; He is with us now. Yet the converse is also true—that the living Christ is to us so wonderful and adorable because He was dead. The fact that He is alive inspires us with strength and hope; but it is by the memory of His death that He is commended to the trust of our burdened consciences and the love of our sympathetic hearts.

[1] Deut. xxi. 22, 23.

[2] "*Crurifragium*, as it was called, consisted in striking the legs of the sufferer with a heavy mallet"—FARRAR, *Life of Christ*, ii., 423.

[3] The words that follow in this paragraph are a reminiscence of a singularly eloquent and powerful passage in a speech of Dr. Maclaren, of Manchester, delivered last year in Edinburgh.

[4] Weiss, however, supposes Psalm xxxiv. 20 to be the reference.

[5] On the symbolism of this phenomenon see the excursus in Westcott's *Gospel of St. John*, pp. 284-86.

[6] *E.g.*, Lange, characteristically.

[7] Stroud in his treatise *On the Physical Cause of the Death of Christ*.

[8] Given in Hanna's *The Last Day of our Lord's Passion*.

CHAPTER XXIII.

THE BURIAL

There is a hard and shallow philosophy which regards it as a matter of complete indifference what becomes of the body after the soul has left it and affects contempt of all funeral ceremonies. But the instincts of mankind are wiser. In ancient times it was considered one of the worst of misfortunes to miss decent burial; and, although this sentiment was mixed with superstition, there was beneath it a healthy instinct. There is a dignity of the body as well as of the soul, especially when it is a temple of the Holy Ghost; and there is a majesty about death which cannot be ignored without loss to the living.[1] It is with a sense of pain and humiliation, as if a dishonour were being done to human nature, that we see a funeral at which everything betokens hurry, shabbiness and slovenliness. On the contrary, the satisfaction is not morbid with which we see a funeral conducted with solemnity and chaste pomp. And, when someone falls whose career has been one of extraordinary achievement and beneficence, and who has become

> On fortune's crowning slope
> The pillar of a nation's hope,
> The centre of a world's desire,

then, as the remains are borne amidst an empire's lamentation to rest "under the cross of gold that shines over river and city," and the tolling bells and echoing cannon sound over hushed London, and the silent masses line the streets, and the learned and the noble stand uncovered around the open grave, it would be a diseased and churlish mind which did not feel the spell of the pageant.

Thus ought the great, the wise and the good to be buried. How then was He buried whom all now agree to call the Greatest, the Wisest and the Best?

I.

The three corpses were taken down towards evening, before the Jewish Sabbath set in, which commenced at sunset. Probably the two robbers were buried on the spot, crosses and all, or they were hurriedly carried off to some obscure and accursed ditch, where the remains of criminals were wont to be unceremoniously thrust underground.

This would have been the fate of Jesus too, had not an unexpected hand interposed. It was the humane custom of the Romans to give the corpses of criminals to their friends, if they chose to ask for them; and a claimant appeared for the body of Jesus, to whom Pilate was by no means loath to grant it.

This is the first time that Joseph of Arimathea appears on the stage of the gospel history; and of his previous life very little is known. Even the town from which he derives his appellation is not known with certainty. The fact that he owned a garden and burying-place in the environs of Jerusalem does not necessarily indicate that he was a resident there; for pious Jews had all a desire to be buried in the precincts of the sacred city; and, indeed, the whole neighbourhood is still honeycombed with tombs.

Joseph was a rich man; and this may have availed him in his application to Pilate. Those who possess wealth or social position or distinguished talents can serve Christ in ways which are not accessible to His humbler followers. Only, before such gifts can be acceptable to Him, those to whom they belong must count them but loss and dung for His sake.

Joseph was a councillor. It has been conjectured that the council of which he was a member was that of Arimathea; but the observation that he "had not consented to the counsel and deed of them," which obviously refers to the Sanhedrim, makes it more than probable that it was of this august body he was a member. No doubt he absented himself deliberately from the meeting at which Jesus was condemned, knowing well beforehand that the proceedings would be utterly painful and revolting to his feelings. For "he was a good man and a just."

We are, however, told more about him: "he waited for the kingdom of God." This is a phrase applied elsewhere also in the New Testament to the devout in Palestine at this period; and it designates in a striking way the peculiarity of their piety. The age was spiritually dead. Religion was represented by the high-and-dry formalism of the Pharisees on the one hand and the cold and worldly scepticism of the Sadducees on the other. In the synagogues the people asked for bread and were offered a stone. The scribes, instead of letting the pure river of Bible truth flow over the land, choked up its course with the sand of their soulless commentary. Yet there are good people even in the worst of times. There were truly pious souls sprinkled up and down Palestine. They were like lights shining here and there, at great intervals, in the darkness. They could not but feel that they were strangers and foreigners in their own age and country, and they lived in the past and the future. The prophets, on whose words they nourished their souls, foretold a good time coming, when on those who sat in darkness there would burst a great light. For this better time, then, they were waiting. They were waiting to hear the voice of prophecy echoing once more through the land and waking the population from its spiritual slumber. They were waiting, above all, for the Messiah, if they might dare to hope that He would come in their days.

Such were the souls among which both John and Jesus found their auditors. All such must have welcomed the voices of the Baptist and his Successor as at least those of prophets who were striving earnestly to deal with the evils of the time. But whether Jesus was He that should come or whether they should look for another, some of them stood in doubt. Among these perhaps was Joseph. He was, it is said, a disciple of Jesus, but secretly, for fear of the Jews. He had faith, but not faith enough to confess Christ and take the consequences. Even during the trial of Jesus he satisfied his conscience by being absent from the meeting of the Sanhedrim, instead of standing up in his place and avowing his convictions.

Such he had been up to this point. But now in the face of danger he identified himself with Jesus. It is interesting to note what it was that brought him to decision. It was the excess of wickedness in his fellow-councillors, who at length went to a stage of violence and injustice which allowed him to hesitate no longer. Complete religious decision is sometimes brought about in this way. Thus, for example, one who has been halting between two opinions, or, at all events, has never had courage enough openly to confess his convictions, may be some day among his fellow-workmen or shopmen, when religion comes up as a topic of conversation and is received with ridicule, Christ's people being sneered at, His doctrines denied, and He Himself blasphemed. But at last it goes too far the silent, half-convinced disciple can stand it no longer; he breaks out in indignant protest and stands confessed as a Christian. In some such way as this must the change of sentiment have taken place in the mind of Joseph. He had to defy the entire Sanhedrim; he was putting himself in imminent peril; but he could hold in no longer; and, casting fear behind his back, he went in "boldly" to Pilate and begged the body of Jesus.

II.

Boldness in confessing Christ is apt to have two results.

On the one hand, it cows adversaries. It is not said that Joseph got himself into trouble by his action on this occasion, or that the Sanhedrim immediately commenced a persecution against him. They were, indeed, in a state of extreme excitement, and they were seventy to one. But sometimes a single bold man can quell much more numerous opposition than even this. It is certain that the consciences of many of them were ill at ease, and they were by no means prepared to challenge to argument on the merits of the case a quiet and resolute man with the elevation of whose character they were all acquainted. It is one of the great advantages of those who stand up for Christ that they have the consciences even of their adversaries on their side.

The other effect of boldness in confessing Christ is that it brings out confession from others who have not had in their own breast enough of fire to make them act, but are heated up to the necessary temperature by example. It seems clear that in this way the example of Joseph evoked the loyalty of Nicodemus.

Nicodemus was of the same rank as Joseph, being a member of the Sanhedrim; and he was a secret disciple. This is not the first time that he appears on the stage of the Gospel history. At the very commencement of the career of Jesus he had been attracted to Him and had gone so far as to seek a private interview; the account of which is one of the most precious component parts of the Gospel and has made tens of thousands not only believers in Christ but witnesses for Him. It had not, however, as much effect on the man to whom it was originally vouchsafed, though it ought to have had. Nicodemus ought to have been one of the earliest followers of the Lord; and his position would have brought weight to the apostolic circle. But he hesitated and remained a secret disciple. On one occasion, indeed, he spoke out: once, when something intolerably unjust was said against Jesus in the Sanhedrim, he interposed the question, "Doth our law judge any man before it hear him and know what he doeth?" But with the angry answer, "Art thou also of Galilee?" he was shouted down; and he held his peace. Doubtless, like Joseph, he absented himself from the meeting of the Sanhedrim at which Jesus was condemned; but the injustice done was so flagrant that he was ready to make a public protest against it. He might not, however, have had the courage of his convictions, had not Joseph shown him the way.

Yet this must be praised in Nicodemus, that he was a growing and improving man. Though he hung back for a time, he came forward at last; and better late than never. It was a happy hour for him when he was brought into contact with Joseph. There are many circles of friends where all are internally convinced and leaning to the right side, and, if only one would come boldly out, the others would willingly follow. The hands of Joseph and Nicodemus met and clasped each other round the body of their Redeemer. There is no love, or friendship, or fellowship like that of those who are united to one another through their connection with Him.

III.

Art has described the burial of our Lord with great fulness of detail, drawing largely on the imagination. It has divided it into several scenes.[2]

There is, first, the Descent from the Cross, in which, besides Joseph and Nicodemus, St. John at least, and sometimes other men, are represented as extracting the nails and lowering the body; while beneath the cross the holy women, among whom the Virgin Mary and Mary Magdalene are prominent, receive the precious burden. Many readers will recall the most famous of such pictures, that by Rubens in the Cathedral at Antwerp—an extremely impressive but too sensuous representation of the scene of busy affection—wherein the corpse is being let down by means of a great white sheet into the hands of the women, who receive it tenderly, one foot resting on the shoulder of the Magdalene.

Then there is what is called the Pieta, or the mourning of the women over the dead body. In this scene the holy mother usually holds the head of her Son in her lap, while the Magdalene clasps His feet and others clasp His hands. Next ensues the Procession to the Sepulchre; and, last of all, there is the Entombment, which is represented in a great variety of forms.

On these scenes the great painters have lavished all the resources of art; but the narrative of the Gospels is brief and unpictorial. The Virgin is not even mentioned; and, although others of the holy women are said to have been there, it is not suggested that they helped in the labour of burial, but only that they followed and marked where He was laid. Joseph and Nicodemus are the prominent actors, though it is reasonable to suppose that they were assisted by their servants; and the soldiers may have lent a hand in disentangling the body.

It was in a new sepulchre, which Joseph had had hewn out of the rock for himself, in order that after death he might lie in the sacred shadow of the city of God, that the Lord was laid. No corpse had ever been placed in it before. This was a great gift to give to an excommunicated and crucified man; and it was a most appropriate one; for it was meet that the pure and stainless One, who had come to make all things new and, though dead, was not to see corruption, should rest in an undefiled sepulchre. Similarly appropriate and suggestive was the new linen cloth, which Joseph bought expressly for the purpose of enwinding the body. Nor was Nicodemus behind in affection and sacrifice. He brought "a mixture of myrrh and aloes, about an hundred pound weight." This may appear an enormous quantity, but custom was very lavish in such gifts; at the funeral of Herod the Great, for example, the spices were carried by five hundred bearers.

The tomb was in a garden—another touch of appropriateness and beauty. The spot does not seem to have been far from the place of execution; but whether it was as near as it is represented to have been in the traditional site may well be doubted. The Church of the Holy Sepulchre includes within its precincts both the Lord's tomb and the hole in the rock in which stood His cross; and the two are only thirty yards apart.[3] But it is highly questionable whether the identification of either is possible. Still, this may be said to be the most famous bit of the entire surface of the globe. Christendom accepted the tradition, which dates from the time of Constantine, and since then pilgrims have flocked to the spot from every land. It was for the possession of this shrine that the Crusades were undertaken, and at the present day the Churches of Christendom fight for a footing in it.

We may have no sympathy with the practice of pilgrimages and little interest in the identification of holy places; but the holy sepulchre cannot but attract the believing heart. It was a practice of the piety of former days to meditate among the tombs. The piety of the present day inclines to more cheerful and, let us hope, not less healthy exercises. But every man with any depth of nature must linger sometimes beside the graves of his loved ones; every man of any seriousness must think sometimes of his own grave. And in such moments what can be so helpful as to pilgrim in spirit to the tomb of Him who said, "I am the resurrection and the life"?

In comparison with the great ones of the earth Jesus had but a humble funeral; yet in the character of those who did Him the last honours it could not have been surpassed; and it was rich in love, which can well take the place of a great deal of ceremony. So at last, stretched out in the new tomb, wherein man had never lain, enwrapped in an aromatic bed of spices and breathed round by the fragrance of flowers, with the white linen round Him and the napkin which hid the wounds of the thorns about His brow, while the great stone which formed the door stood between Him and the world, He lay down to rest. It was evening, and the Sabbath drew on; and the Sabbath of His life had come. His work was completed; persecution and hatred could not reach Him any more; He was where the wicked cease from troubling and the weary are at rest.

[1] The most beautiful thing ever said about the bodies of the dead is in the Shorter Catechism: "And their bodies, being still united to Christ, do rest in their graves till the resurrection."

[2] On these and similar details see *The Life of our Lord as exemplified in Works of Art*, by Mrs. Jameson (completed by Lady Eastlake).

[3] Many interesting details in Ross's *Cradle of Christianity*.

Milton Keynes UK
Ingram Content Group UK Ltd.
UKHW030741071024
449371UK00006B/663